What does it take to sustain and shepherd a congregation in the critical moments after the Holy Spirit works with power? From his experience of an extraordinary season of revival over thirty years ago, Pastor Humrichous offers principles to steward Christ's presence and activity on an ongoing basis. This book is the culmination of a lifetime of reflection and pastoral wisdom.

Del Fehsenfeld
Senior Editor Revive Magazine
Pastoral Services Director
Life Action Ministry

There are several teachers in life, from people and books, from life experience and certainly from the Holy Spirit. Pastor Joe has gleaned from each of these in his journey of life and faith. In his book, The Life of the Vine in the Soul of the Church, he passes along to us a compilation of what he has learned on his personal journey. He is a gifted communicator, both from the pulpit and as a writer. I consider myself blessed to serve with him and learn from him as Jesus and the church are the greatest passions of his life.

Andy Harkleroad
Co-Pastor First Baptist Church
Covington, IN

Does the potential of having Christ present and in charge of your life and ministry fascinate you? It should! And within the pages of this book you will find the story of one pastor's transformation from life in the power of the flesh into a life led by Christ "obviously present and actively in charge." Here is the heart of dynamic Christian living and of a healthy, vibrant church.

Pastor Joe Humrichous, a Barnabas to pastors, shares his personal journey of faith and timeless biblical truths that has already helped countless others to understand that life outside the Vine will only be dry and fruitless. With an emphasis on praying with Christ present and in charge, he demonstrates how the spirit of revival can live in a church whose soul is transformed by the life of the Vine. A must-read for ministry leaders!

Mike Hohenstein
Administrative Elder
First Baptist Church
Covington, IN

This is a story of a pastor who learned the difference between doing ministry for God and letting God do ministry through him. It is a story about learning to depend upon the Vine to supply everything that a branch needs. It is a story of moving from an activity centered church to a "Presence of Christ" centered church. As you read this book, give thanks to God for how He graciously teaches His servants that it is not about us, but it is all about Christ and His power setting a church free.

Dr. Erwin W. Lutzer
Senior Pastor
Moody Church
Chicago, IL

Jesus Christ is building His church. Sadly our ministry efforts do not always line up with that great truth. The author's candid description of his own growth in understanding the Lord's plan serves as a much needed warning to young pastors of the pitfall of misplaced emphasis in ministry. The practical insights that follow are of immeasurable value to anyone who seeks to redirect their service to give the Lord His rightful place in the church.

Art Nuernberg
Pastoral Director
EI School of Biblical Training
Greenville, SC

I met Pastor Joe Humrichous because of an extraordinary spiritual revival – one of Life Action's ministry teams went to a small town in

Indiana for a week long meeting that didn't finish until six weeks later! Thousands of lives and two separate communities were radically impacted. This man saw the fire of revival and smoke is still on his clothes!

Byron Paulus
Director of Life Action Ministries

Joe Humrichous has been a dear friend for over forty years. This book chronicles his personal journey of growing in grace and in the knowledge of our Lord and Savior Jesus Christ. I have walked with Joe for many miles on this journey and can validate the truths he proclaims. If you apply these truths from this book, it will change your life.

David E. Rowland
President of Union Gospel Press

PRACTICAL – POWERFUL – PERTINENT! There is a "where the rubber meets the road" account of a pastor's struggle and search for the reality of Christ – first of all in his own personal life – and then in his desire to see the outworking of Christ truly becoming the life of the church. The thorough biblical presentation of this basic reality is a "breath of fresh air" in the midst of the stifling bondages of many man-made efforts to move the church in our day. This is a "must read" for pastors, ministerial students and Christian workers everywhere!

Louis Sutera, Revivalist
Canadian Revival Fellowship

Brother Joe, I commend and thank you for doing a great service to the body of Christ in writing this book. Your transparent personal story of being delivered from being a busy man in ministry into Christ becoming center of your life and actively in charge in your local churches comes out loud and clear. In an age where easy "believism" is too often purported, this sorely needed and overlooked message is so timely. More specifically I consider it a "must" read for those who aspire to or are directly involved in full-time pastoral and church ministries. May those who seriously implement this message with its sound biblical truths find themselves delivered from the devastation of serving God in the energy of the flesh, thus becoming candidates for genuine biblical revival. I am grateful to have had a small part in witnessing this as a reality in your personal life and ministry.

Ralph Sutera, Revivalist
Canadian Revival Fellowship

The Life of the Vine in the Soul of the Church is both a narrative and theological story. You cannot unwind these two elements – narrative and theology – because they are inextricably bound together in Joe's life. His story is woven throughout the biblical teaching in a way that both Baby Boomer and Millennial will resonate. His narrative draws you into that story until ultimately, finally, hungry, you discover the story in your own life. How like Christ! I highly encourage pastors, church leaders, and anyone who thirsts for both transformation and revival to read Joe's experience and wisdom. You will detect Christ's power within your outreach and leadership.

Dr. Paul Utnage

THE VINE AND THE CHURCH

7 Stewardships of Revival

By Joe Humrichous

Please note that all Scripture quotes come from the authorized King James translation of the Bible.

Shepherd's Publishing, LLC
515 6th Street
Box 267
Covington, IN 47932
765 793 2177

Cover art/photography by: Sunny Wilderman

Book layout/design by
  Arcand Publishing, *a division of Word Services Unlimited*
  loralee@wordservicesunlimited.com
  wordservicesunlimited.com

Printed in the United States.

Dedication

To my dad – Gordon Walden Humrichous
> A farmer whose godly, humble ways were life lessons which laid the foundation for my ministry.

To my pastor – Dr. Wesley Potter
> Who carried my picture in his wallet and claimed me for the Lord until I was born again.

To Sarah Merry
> Who unconditionally loved a young pastor and wife and introduced the Christ-life to me. Forever grateful.

To my mentor – Oliver Price
> Whose eight-word statement "Jesus Christ Obviously Present and Actively in Charge" focused my understanding of revival and Christ centered-church ministry. He followed this definition with 22 years of mentorship and partnership.

Acknowledgments

To Teresa, my beloved wife, my "Indiana Princess" and gift from God, who worked diligently by my side and administered this project. I love you.

To Andy Harkleroad and Mike Hohenstein, my comrades who coached and encouraged me to get the words on paper and were always interested in my project. What a blessing you are.

To Dave Rowland, my life-long ministry friend, whose expertise and servant spirit always gave me ideas and hope for the next step.

To the brotherhood of men and women with whom I have had the privilege of serving with over the last 50 years. Your friendships are a treasure. You know who you are. Your servant hands were used by Christ to make ministry happen.

To my children who have taken the message of this book seriously and practiced it in your homes.

To Loralee at Word Services Unlimited for her readiness and competence. You are a joy to work with.

To Marsha Wilkinson, whose last minute red pencil propelled us to the finish.

Table of Contents

Foreword

As the author was quick to point out, this book contains nothing new. He is just reminding us of things we already know, and oh, how we need to be reminded, lest at any time we should let them slip. Part of the curse is that we forget things we should remember and remember the things we should forget. The Apostle Peter felt he would be negligent if he didn't remind people of things they already knew. Hearing things again only helps to further establish us in the truth.

I am so thankful Joe included his testimony and candidly shared some of his ups and downs, victories and defeats, successes and failures. Oh, how necessary these realistic growing pains are if we are to mature as believers in Jesus. Hardships often have a way of grooming us for greater works. I was captivated as I tracked along with him in his journey of faith. It was deeply moving as he told of the faithfulness of his Savior and His desire to be obviously present and actively involved in his life and ministry.

For some, these will be new insights. For others, they will be a new depth to old truths will be provided. Whichever, they are words that will refresh your soul and strengthen your faith. *The Life of the Vine in the Soul of the Church* is about abiding in Jesus. It is a balanced view of revival and the stewardships of revival. We would do well to know "When the church is revived, so is the devil" (Jonathon Edwards, 1703-1758). I was both convicted and inspired as I read his words on prayer – that place where God and human beings meet. Contact with deity is a life-giving essential for the soul of every believer in Jesus, regardless of his seniority in the faith. What a blessing to track with Joe as he takes the reader through a practical and balanced view of grace, faith, worship, warfare, and choice. These timeless truths are what go into making up the life of Jesus in the soul of His people. I think the Holy Spirit is pleased with this work and pray He will use it in the lives of many as He has in mine. This will be an annual read for me to remind me of the things I already know, lest I forget what manner of man I am.

Itinerant Preacher – Tom Harmon
Founder of Faithful Men of Michigan

Introduction

At the expense of sounding too pious, I wrote this book for Jesus. For too long, I did not give Him His proper place in church building. I am sorry. He knew where I was in my understanding of things and was patient and intentional in performing His work in me. I'm sure He has more to teach me.

I'm not trying to bring back any glory days. Jesus is now! Therefore, revival is now for those who cherish Him in their lives and in their church.

Section 4 is the central concept laid out in stewardships. To me it is much more than an outline. It traces our ministry response to the life and activity of the Vine. The ways of Christ in this section have been grafted deeply in my soul over many years of study, trial, and observation. This is not a "How to do it" book. It is a "How He does it" book; it is from my heart a spiritual act of worship to Jesus. I live these truths as a leader every day in ministry. They hold me. To Him be glory in the church by Christ Jesus.

The Heart of This Book

At the heart of this book lie two simple motivations. First, I want to chronicle part of my journey with God for my children and grandchildren. Leaving a legacy of the faithfulness of God will hopefully help to pass the faith along. This chronicle will also give context to other friends and pastoral readers who may be more interested in the corporate application to the church. I will be as brief as possible on personal details in order to move the narrative along and yet maintain the core truth of the **life of the Vine in the soul of God's servant**.

Secondly, <u>I want to build a bridge</u> for God's pastoral servants who labor in the local church. The question at hand is, <u>**"How can I allow Christ to build His church like He promised and still maintain responsible leadership?"**</u> The extremes in styles of leadership range from being "graced" out and doing nothing to micromanaging every aspect of a local ministry. From Scripture and personal experience, I am convinced there is a spirit-directed cooperation with Jesus that will glorify God, energize the laborers and see a harvest of lives for the Kingdom.

These are truths I did not know 48 years ago when I first entered local church ministry. We only know what we have seen and heard. Sadly, I had never grasped the concept of <u>the life of the Vine in the soul of the church,</u> but when I did, ministry became a grace adventure with lasting fruit. What a difference! I never want to go back. If you are new in ministry, especially the pastorate, my prayer is that these concepts will start you off with the right focus. It's a lot more fun and much more fruitful.

In Him,
Joe

How to Read This Book

To free busy readers who prefer to cut to the chase and find the bottom line of the seven stewardships, let me suggest you read strategically as follows:

- Chapter 2 "True Salvation" – This is the time when my life really began to change.
- Chapter 8 "Crash and Burn" – This chronicles my brokenness and personal revival.
- Chapter 9 "Back to the Bible" – This secures all experience in the Scripture.
- Chapter 16 "Oliver Price" – This focused my definition of revival.
- Chapter 17 "Frowning Providence" – This relates God's sovereign placement of my home.
- Chapter 18 "Corporate Prayer" – This drives all ministry of the Head (Christ) to the body.
- Chapters 19-25 "7 Stewardships" – This relates our responses to God's activity.

"Builder of Bridges"

An old man, traveling a lone highway
Came at the evening cold and gray
To a chasm deep and wide.

The old man crossed in the twilight dim,
The sullen stream held no fear for him.
But he turned when he reached the other side,
And built a bridge to span the tide.

"Old man," cried a fellow pilgrim near,
"You are wasting your strength with building here;
Your journey will end with the ending day,
And you never again will pass this way.

You have crossed the chasm deep and wide.
Why build you a bridge at eventide?"
And the builder raised his old gray head,
"Good friend, on the path I have come," he said.
"There followeth after me today,
A youth whose feet will pass this way.
This stream, which has been as naught to me,
To that fair-haired boy may a pitfall be.
He, too, must cross in the twilight dim.
Good friend, I am building this bridge for him."

Unknown

SECTION ONE

The Life of the Vine
in the Soul of the Preacher

1
The Farm

*"The lines are fallen unto me
In pleasant places; yea, I have
A goodly heritage."* –Psalm 16:6

*"You can take the boy out
Of the country but —"*

My dad and mom crossed the cattle guard at the end of our lane in August 1946. I was six months old. Dad had just returned home from the service where he had been shot down over Germany during WWII, and he was very happy to drive his '39 Ford with his young bride and new baby boy up the lane to what was, at one time, his grandparents' home. This was to be the "home place" until I left at age 19. It was to me a boy's paradise on earth.

My youthful perspective of the farm was that of happiness, fun, and encouragement. Even hard work was presented as an industry to be embraced and enjoyed. The adults actually convinced me that this "sweat equity" would make a man out of me and that I would be able to enjoy the satisfaction of a job well done. My dad was always clear about "first things first" and "finish what you start." I loved him. I loved his teachings. I loved his humble spirit. I loved how he was willing to work alongside us and be first to tackle the hardest task.

Exciting things happened on the farm all the time. New lambs, calves, and pigs were born and were sometimes hand-fed in the kitchen. New chickens were hatched, and sometimes Grandpa would go to the Amish country and buy a new workhorse just for the fun of pulling a hay wagon. New or "new to us" farm machinery would be bought to improve the operation, but the most delightful things in my young life were the people and the context they gave to everything. Their humorous stories, common sense, and Scripture quotes always seemed to keep things in perspective. I felt very secure about life with them.

Every family member donned unique personalities that contributed a full expression of what family should be. They were joyful, hardworking, safe, resourceful, content, church-going people, and they were very encouraging to me as the oldest grandchild. I can truly testify with the psalmist that I have a goodly heritage. **Through my family, the Vine (Jesus) was surrounding my life.** I would recommend my home for any boy or girl, but evidently **there was one dimension of Christian living that was not understood – at least it was never related clearly. Thus. I was developing a subtle and wicked way and didn't know it. God would radically deal with this later.**

> *"Search me, O God, and know*
> *My heart: try me, and know*
> *My thoughts: And see if*
> *There be any wicked way in me,*
> *And lead me in the way*
> *Everlasting"* –Psalm 139:23, 24

2

True Salvation

"And this is the life eternal, that they might know Thee, the only true God, and Jesus Christ, whom Thou hast sent." –John 17:3

September 8, 1965 – the day I willingly, by grace, changed ruling spiritual governments from the world, the flesh, and the Devil – to the Father, the Son, and the Holy Spirit.

My salvation came after years of labor pains. Some would think it unwise to put the date of one's salvation in a testimony like this for fear that some would depend on a date or some might doubt because they didn't know a date of spiritual birth. I understand their concern so let me be clear that Jesus Christ, not a prayer or a decision or a date, is the object of my faith. This particular day in the fall of 1965 marked the end of my conscious struggle against God and the beginning of my saying yes to Him. Here's the story.

Life continued on the farm with great enrichment from my home, our church, and my two-room country school, all within three miles of each other. Home was great. I was learning basic skills for general farm work and felt good using them side by side with my dad and whoever else he had working with us. Church was a community of families gathering to worship. I felt secure in their sense of doing right and respecting God. School was great. Again, it was like family. Our PTA meetings were packed with parents who were interested in their kids' lives. When I was 10 years old, Dad and Mom announced that they were expecting another baby. On July 6, 1956, my brother Jim was born. Life was good.

My mom told me that when I was five, I had asked Jesus into my heart, but I didn't remember it, and by the time I was 13, I began to show definite signs of independence, selfishness, and rebellion. At age 14, I was thrown from the tractor I was driving and the back wheel ran over my head. By God's mercy, my life was spared. I do remember when Pastor Wesley Potter came to the emergency room to comfort my family. He spoke to me. "Joe, things don't look good. I just need to know one thing – if you die tonight, will you go to heaven – do you know Jesus?"

I proudly and disgustingly said, "Yeah." **That one personal experience has taught me that life-threatening circumstances alone are not enough to draw a person to Christ. We must have grace.** That accident actually took place on the eve of my 8th grade graduation from the country school. After 15 days in the hospital and a full summer to recover, I was off to high school – in town. In my mind, this would be a major adjustment.

High school offered all the things you would expect. I continued to go to church with my family though we had moved to a different church. It was a strong Bible-teaching church with several young people as well as a close association with a fellowship of churches that supported and ran a local Christian camp. I entered a full-scale personal war in the proverbial struggle between the church and the world. I loved people on both sides of the struggle.

Let me pause right here and say how very grateful I am today for those pastors, workers, and comrades who continued to display attractive Christ-like attitudes that I could clearly see. They were truly instruments of grace used by God. Every time I cross paths with Romans 8:29, I think of them. "For whom He did foreknow, He also did predestinate to be conformed to the image of His Son... The word "foreknow" here means to know by experience. In other words, God is personally involved in the process of our coming to Him. As I look back, I see many persons who were God's fingers as His hands brought me to Himself. I am also humbled and so very grateful. Let me give a verse to you as His laborer right now.

"*Therefore, my beloved brethren, be ye steadfast, unmovable, always abounding in the work of the Lord, forasmuch as ye know that your labour is not in vain in the Lord*" (I Cor. 15:58).

That one personal experience has taught me that life-threatening circumstances alone are not enough to draw a person to Christ. We must have grace.

I continued on with very strong influences on both sides of the struggle. At this stage in my life, I was able to get away with being eagerly accepted by both camps. I knew how to behave. I knew how to perform. In the world, I could become an honor student, be respected by my peers, and excel in athletics. In the church, I could lead youth events, sing solos, and even give some Bible devotions on certain occasions. But Joe was lord, not Jesus.

In my carnal mind, I was in no way subject to the law of God. It is crystal clear to me how people can do many wonderful works and yet have the Lord say, "Depart from Me, ye that work iniquity (lawlessness)" (Matt. 7:23). In my hypocritical misery, Jesus was asking me, "Joe, why do you call me Lord and do not the things which I say?" (Luke 6:46).

Upon graduation from high school, I looked like a respectable, church-going, young citizen who would graduate with honors and enter the workforce in some field of agriculture. My dad had clearly told me that the farm could not support another adult and that I should look for other employment. I enrolled in college, intending to pursue a career in agricultural chemistry. My family, my pastor, and my church friends encouraged me to go to Bible College. I couldn't imagine leaving the world of cars, girls, and sports for the prudish lifestyle of purity. I was offered a full ride basketball scholarship to the local junior college, and that became my way out of the prison of a Bible education and the type of life it would require.

My 19th year was the worst year and the best year of my life. I hated junior college. Basketball season was a bust with the team winning only one game. My cars kept blowing up, thereby increasing my debt load. My classmates headed off in different directions, and I certainly wasn't suited to be a fit husband for any girl. I quit junior college after the ball season and went to work for a typewriter company. God had lovingly and systematically brought me to the end of myself – how gracious.

I sold my beloved '57 Chevy to my girlfriend and left for Bible College, chauffeured by my parents in their boring '61 Chevy sedan. That first week, while under the preaching of a great biblical orator and surrounded by godly and lively peers, I knelt on a locker room floor with the rest of the soccer team and from my heart said silently to God alone, "I will do this – I believe You." By grace I changed governments, and God took over. Thankfully I have never been sorry and never turned back, but I had no idea how much work had to be done by God in me. It was a new beginning. **The Vine had entered my life.**

"For we are His workmanship,
Created in Christ Jesus unto
Good works, Which God hath
Before ordained that we should
Walk in them." –Ephesians 2:10

"And Jesus said unto them,
Come ye after me, and I
Will make you to become
Fishers of men." –Mark 1:17

3
A Life's Verse

"That I may know Him, and the
Power of His resurrection, and
The fellowship of His sufferings,
Being made conformable unto
His death;" –Philippians 3:10

"The Christian life and ministry can be fraught with
many noble and subtle substitutes for Jesus." – jch
"Messages should be good news, not just good advice."
– jch

Over the span of my 19 years sitting in preaching services, I had
experienced many "moved but not changed" moments. Often I was
nudged by God about the rightness of the gospel message. One time
shortly after the tractor accident, I responded to the altar call during
our fall revival meeting at church. On the way to a counseling room,
my mom saw me and asked what I was doing. I said, "I think I need
to get saved." She said, "Oh, you're just tired." That set me back a
bit in moving forward with clear repentance and faith. To this day
I'm not sure why she did that. Perhaps because I was looked upon
as somewhat of a young leader – to then admit that I wasn't even
saved would have been an embarrassment to her. A word to parents:
let God deal with your kids no matter how awkward or painful it
may be for you. Let Him work.

These types of stirrings would often occur at camp. Nearly every
summer at the last campfire service, I would rededicate the life I

didn't have. Even though these decisions didn't stick, they were used by God to witness to my spirit that there was something outside of my life and my lifestyle that was real. He was cultivating a longing that I could not deny.

During the opening meetings of my new Christian college semester, a similar thing happened, but this time I was alone and away from all previous influences and could follow through. On the eve of my conversion, I found myself being drawn again to respond to the message. I was taken to a side room by an older student named Bob Fuller. Again, I identified the need to rededicate. He had never known me before, so he listened graciously, gave me some standard verses, and then we prayed together. After praying he asked me, "Joe, do you have a life verse?" I didn't know what that meant, so he clarified with the idea that it was a special verse that you felt somewhat outlined the direction of your life. He suggested Philippians 3:10 as one for me. He read it and asked, "What do you think?" I said, "Sounds good to me." **In my courteous ignorance, the Vine was marking my path before me.** I was to become a child of God the next day, and this verse defined my morphing to maturity.

Here it is:

> *That I may know Him,*
> *And the power of His resurrection,*
> *And the fellowship of His sufferings,*
> *Being made conformable unto His*
> *Death;* –Philippians 3:10

Fifty years later, I'm still learning what it means. Later, I will show you that these words are at the core of my life's message and the heart of this book.

4
Call to Preach

*"In hope of eternal life which God, that cannot lie,
promised before the world began; but hath in due times
manifested His Word through preaching, which is
committed unto me according to the commandment
of God our Savior;* –Titus 1:2, 3

A message prepared in the mind – reaches the mind
A message prepared in the heart – reaches the heart
A message prepared in the life – reaches the life
–Del Fehsenfeld Jr.

In the fall of 1966, one year after my conversion, God called me to the ministry of preaching. I had developed the habit of reading my Bible daily. While sitting at my student desk in my dorm room, I started reading the Book of Titus. In verse 3, Paul mentioned that God actually manifested His Word through preaching which he said "is committed unto me." When I read that phrase, it stood out, captured my attention, and repeated in my mind like a broken record. This thought from the Word held me and began to hem me in. Is God actually calling me to preach? In what capacity? Pastor? Missionary?

In order to test its authenticity, I would lay it down for a few days and then come back to it. The call seemed to stay and desire arose. For several weeks, this was an inner dialogue between God and me alone. One day I decided to put this call to a public test with this prayer to the Father. "Lord if this is real, I will do it; I will go anywhere You ask, first come, first serve – as long as I can get there. I will never ask for a dime, but You must be my booking agent." It was a defining moment. All this time, these years, etc., I have enjoyed watching God book me and provide for me and my family. It has been a miracle ride of grace. God has been so faithful. Sometimes I have stood in front of audiences and been able to say, "I am only here by the sovereign placement of God." Once, while speaking in Brazil, South America, I heard an elder missionary statesman say, "Volunteering because of a need will get you to the mission field, but a call from God will keep you there." That spoke to me, and this grace of His inward call has kept me preaching. To this day, I love unpacking a passage, getting the big idea, making it palatable for the hearers, and delivering it in an interesting way.

I became a real fan of expository preaching. Haddon W. Robinson, Biblical Preaching, calls it: "Expository Preaching is the communication of a biblical concept derived from and transmitted through a historical, grammatical and literary study of a passage in its context, which the Holy Spirit first applies to the personality and experience of the preacher, then through him to his hearers."

Prior to this call, you must understand that my opinion of preachers was not good. Surely preaching would be the way of boredom and poverty. Not so. It continues to be a great adventure of God enjoyment, lined with beautiful Spirit-filled people who have lavished me with generous, unconditional love. God has made His callings and election sure in my life. Truly His callings are without repentance, and I have no regrets for saying yes to His tug to preach.

My advisors suggested I start by preparing for the pastorate and then be alert to God's further direction. So, I majored in Bible and minored in pastorology and Greek. I started letting people know of my call, and opportunities began to come in – rest homes, rescue missions, prisons, and youth rallies. **There was, however, something about preaching no one told me. It would be radically introduced**

by God at a strategic time some years later. God was patient as I continued to hone my preaching skills and use them as He directed. **The Vine was anointing the branch for preaching. Pruning would come soon.**

5
College Days

"*Being confident of this very thing,*
That He which hath begun a good
Work in you will perform it until
The day of Jesus Christ." –Philippians 1:6

"Has this world been so kind to you
That you should leave with regret?
There are better things ahead than
Any we leave behind." –C.S. Lewis

It would be an understatement for me to say that my four years at Bible College were formative years. God was demolishing the old and bringing in the new. From the fall of 1965 until the spring of 1969, my life went through what seemed like major surgery with no anesthetic. I became a true believer, met the lady I would marry, called to preach, became a public speaker, was thrust into a pastorology tract of study, and became a youth pastor in a local church 25 miles from campus. None of this was what I had in mind when I left home, God was directing my steps. [Growing up for 10 years as the only child made me very self-centered. Growing up on the farm in the country made me very homesick. I like privacy which was crushed by dorm life.] Working to support myself and carrying a full class load in school was a stretch.

God was overhauling my moral impurities, my temporal values, and my pride. All of this is clear to me now. At the time, then it was like hand-to-hand combat in the shadows of a dimly lit room. Bible truth was taught and caught, and those little flickering lamps slowly but surely became a light to the path. There was one spiritual battle and birth after another as "pilgrim made progress"

DiAnne Pehl was God's choice for me to marry. She was a farmer's daughter from southern Minnesota. When we met, our spirits were kindred, and we talked freely for hours. God was transforming my relationship with the opposite sex, and I knew marriage was a calling. I felt drawn and called to her. In many ways, we were very different, especially in our walk with the Lord. She, along with her twin sister, DeLoris, had trusted Jesus at age seven. They had submitted to Christ, studied the Scriptures, seriously walked with the Lord through high school, and stayed pure for their mate.

DiAnne played the piano well, but her passion was not music. Rather it was for children and the Scriptures. God gave us four children, and she was very diligent about making sure our family memorized Scripture. Her favorite passage was Psalm 27.

She felt very called to be a pastor's wife. Her journals as a young girl revealed her prayers for a godly mate. I was about 7 months old in the Lord when we began to relate. She actually taught me to read my Bible and underline with a #2 red grading pencil, which I still do today. Early on she wrote poems for my messages and pointed out good ideas for sermons. She wrote this piece as an expression of her heart early on.

"The Bench"

I have an orange crate box with
A board upon its top.
It's out behind the house in a
Wonderful little spot.
It's here I meet my Saviour
And talk with Him awhile.
He gives me blessings o'er
And brings a heartfelt smile.
This box it seems to me
Is sanctified by God.
But I know it's who I meet there
That makes the place seem odd.

–DiAnne Faye Pehl, 1957 – Age 13

The Vine was providing me with a mate – a counterpart with the same calling.

We were married from June 23, 1967, until November 16, 2002, when DiAnne's battle with cancer took her life. God had been glorified in that battle. I bought hundreds of grading pencils and had them in baskets for those who attended her memorial service. **Her life's message was "Love the Lord, love the Word, and love the children."**

During our college days as a couple, we were given grace to persevere. The college actually split while we were there because of personality struggles amongst strong leaders. Many of my colleagues went to the new school, but my dad's counsel was to stay where we started; so we did. That was right for us.

Preaching became a very big deal to me. Preaching was emphasized by my mentors, admired by my colleagues and modeled by chapel speakers. It seemed that the success of my church or ministry depended on the dynamic delivery of a sermon. How well a man could preach seemed to be the measure of his ministry and character. So I strapped it on – homiletics, pulpit speech, pitch, pause, pace, point, punch! Bless God, I had-er down! **I would learn something very different later.**

While writing this, I found the printed message I used in the annual "Preacher Boys" contest. It was homiletically sound but tragically insincere. God in His unfailing mercy seemed to use these exhibitions of smoke and mirrors to help the kids in my youth group. By grace, a better day was coming. To be honest, I still love to preach the Word but with a different heart.

*H*er life's message would be, "Love the Lord, love the Word, and love the children."

> *"Preach the Word; be instant*
> *In season, out of season;*
> *Reprove, rebuke, exhort with*
> *All long suffering and doctrine."* –II Timothy 4:2

6
Seminary Days

"The wind bloweth where it listeth,
And thou hearest the sound thereof,
But canst not tell whence it cometh,
And whither it goeth: so is every one
That is born of the Spirit." –John 3:8

"Blessed assurance, Jesus is mine!
O what a foretaste of glory divine!
Heir of salvation, purchase of God,
Born of His Spirit, washed in His blood."
                                        –Fanny J. Crosby

God was so gracious during those college days. Our parents were supportive and cheered us on. By the time graduation rolled around in the spring of 1969, we were expecting our first child, and I was enjoying a fruitful ministry as a youth pastor in a local church. Even though I was learning the ropes of feeding God's sheep, I still felt very strongly that I had a lot of maturing to do and a lot more to learn. So we packed up and left Owatonna, Minnesota, for Chattanooga, Tennessee. By now, DiAnne was nine months pregnant with our daughter, Johanna. When we announced to her parents that we were headed for Chattanooga for more schooling, her dad said, "Joe, you don't need more schooling, you need more sense!" He was wrong on the first part but right on the second. Fortunately, he blessed us by giving us his 1956 Ford farm truck for the 1,000-mile journey. Its top speed was 45-50 miles per hour. We drove the first 500 miles separately, and then my parents and little brother joined the journey and drove the truck the rest of the way. They thought they were big-time movers. Country was soon meet city. By the way, on that trip, we ate in this quaint country restaurant we liked – it was called Cracker Barrel. They were just getting started that year and weren't sure about the future of their business!

During those years, my spiritual boat really began to rock. It was a change of culture – north to south. It was a change of scenery – country to city. It was a change of family – farther from home with a new baby. It was larger – new friends, more expenses, harder studies, but grace made a way. Many days I felt broke, exhausted from work, overwhelmed with studies, neglectful of my new little family, and very homesick for the farm. **God was using everyday responsibilities and surroundings to purge the branch, but I was too naive biblically to know what was going on. God was dealing with my wicked way.**

I didn't know anyone, so there were no invitations to preach. I missed preaching. By the fall of 1970, I had made friends through my classes. One man was a pastor in a church 50 miles to the south just across the line in north Georgia. He invited me to be their music and youth director. We had a great time, and right away God began to bless and give us a local church family where we could feel at home.

While studying at seminary, and serving our new church, I began to have some old temptations return from my unsaved years, and for the first time, I began to doubt my salvation. For five years I was so confident in my faith and assured in God's call, but now I became almost plagued with doubts and insecurity. I had thoughts of suicide just to know the surety of it all. Needless to say, you can see the hand of the deceiver all over that thinking. One day in chapel, we were singing "Blessed Assurance." I was surrounded by men who were standing up tall and singing with all their might, "Blessed Assurance, Jesus is mine, O what a foretaste of glory divine." Tears filled my eyes. I was miserable, broke, tired, unsure. I was not singing. My heart was saying, "God, please help." I knew the verses to quote. I needed the Spirit to bear witness and bring them off the page.

God was using everyday responsibilities and surroundings to purge the branch but I was too naive biblically to know what was going on. God was dealing with my wicked way.

Around that same time, one of the boys in our youth group drowned. Nearly every Sunday afternoon I would play basketball with the guys. I loved sports, and God often used basketball to help me relate and engage the kids. This particular day, our lunch went overtime, and I was late getting back. The guys got hot and headed for the neighbor's pond. One of them cramped and drown. Joyfully, he had received Christ just weeks before and was growing like a weed spiritually. It was a very sad time for our church, but we sorrowed as a family that had hope because of his earlier conversion.

I was then faced with a huge challenge. The family asked me to assist in the memorial service with the pastor. No one knew of my struggle with assurance. I had kept it to myself. How could a God-called preacher and seminary student admit to such a fundamental flaw? **I was now put by God in a squeeze play for authenticity. I could not fake this funeral message.**

Needing to hear from God, I got alone in our little youth center apartment and knelt down at our old green chair. I begged God to show me Scripture and assure my heart one way or the other. The only Scripture that focused was John 3. I opened my Bible and reviewed this old familiar text, and there it was, something I had never seen before. John 3:8. Jesus said to Nicodemus, "The wind bloweth where it listeth, and thou hearest the sound thereof, but canst not tell whence it cometh, and whither it goeth: so is every one that is born of the Spirit." I got it – for the first time, I got it. Jesus was making a point to Nicodemus that the work of the Holy Spirit in salvation was like the wind. It cannot be controlled or understood, but we can believe it and see its effects. Salvation was of God alone. It was both a miracle and a mystery. This was the life of God in the soul of man, and it could not be understood through mental analysis. It was to be embraced by child-like faith. I was set free, preached the memorial service, and enjoyed a brand new understanding of the mystery Paul referred to in Colossians 1:27, "Christ in you, the hope of glory." I often say now that **I am not a mystic, but I am trying to explore this great mystery of Christ in me.**

This reality was the chief treasure I gleaned from the seminary years. It would be tested, expanded, and applied again and again in the years ahead. Around that time I became familiar with John 15 and began to understand more about this Vine.

7
The Call to Pastorate #1

"As they ministered to the Lord, and fasted, the Holy Ghost said, 'Separate me Barnabas and Saul for the work whereunto I have called them'." –Acts 13:2

"If you can explain what's going on, God didn't do it."
–Bob Cook (past Youth for Christ president)

As seminary came to an end (May 1972), we found ourselves in a good place. The Lord allowed me to pass all my classes, finish my papers, and pay my school bill. God had also blessed us with a son Jason, so now we had a little girl almost 3 and a little boy of 7 months. By grace I was understanding more and more about the mystery of salvation, yet there seemed to be a hunger for something I couldn't quite grasp. We had felt led to leave the church where I served as youth pastor for the last few months of seminary in order to finish well. I loved my job driving tractor-trailer for Roadway Express. It paid well, I was home more, and I enjoyed jamming gears making deliveries throughout the countryside. Often my fellow students would ask what I was going to do after graduation. I didn't know; I just wanted to finish well and then look at my options. During my last week of school, just before graduation, the head deacon from the church we had taken a break from called. Their pastor, whom I had served under, had just resigned, and they wanted us to consider coming back and becoming the Senior Pastor. I was 26. We set up a meeting, and they all came to our very modest apartment that week. They were kind and graciously expressed appreciation for our ministry with their youth and encouraged us to pray about returning. I was respectful, and with lip service, agreed to pray, but my heart sank at the thought. Truck driving actually sounded better – more free.

My memories of the place were somewhat dark because of my struggles with salvation and the death of my young friend. I had hoped to go someplace with a fresh start closer to home.

After graduation we took a trip back home to visit parents. While there, I was reading, praying, and waiting on the Lord for His direction. It was my habit to read systematically through books of the Bible. I was also recalling my encounter with the Lord back at the time of my original call to preach. "I will go anywhere You ask but You must be my booking agent." My Bible reading that day fell on Matthew 21. Jesus was speaking.

"— a certain man had two sons; and he came to the first, and said, Son, go work today in my vineyard. He answered and said I will not: but afterward he repented, and went. And he came to the second, and said likewise. And he answered and said, I go, sir: and went not. *Whether of the twain did the will of his father —*" (Matt. 21:28-31). The verses seemed to jump off the page at that moment, identifying me as the one who said "No" first and later went doing the will of his Father. As I related this private time with DiAnne, she agreed that God was in this. Shortly afterward, with the help of the people from the church, we made the move. Little did I know that through that move, I would learn the lesson of a lifetime. It would be painful, but it would become my deepest treasure and life message. **How grateful I am to God for His leadership through the quiet reading of His Word. Clearly God was at work because at the time I had no explanation. Here the Vine would reveal and replace my wicked way.**

"Obedience"
George MacDonald

I said: "Let me walk in the fields."
He said: "Nay, walk in the town."
I said: "There are no flowers there."
He said: "No flowers but a crown."

I said: "But the sky is black;
There is nothing but noise and din."
And He wept as He led me back –
"There is more." He said: "There is sin."

I said,: "But the air is thick,
And fogs are veiling the sun."
He answered: "Yet souls are sick,
And souls in the dark undone!"

I said: "I shall miss the light,
And friends will miss me, they say."
He answered: "Choose tonight
If I am to miss you, or they."

I pleaded for time to be given.
He said: "Is it hard to decide?
It will not seems hard in heaven
To have followed the steps of your Guide."

I cast one look at the field,
Then set my face to the town;
He said: "My child, do you yield?
Will you leave the flowers for the crown?"

Then into His hand went mine;
And into my heart came He;
And I walk in a light divine,
The path I had feared to see.

8

Crash and Burn, the Turning Point

"I am the Vine, ye are the branches:
He that abideth in Me, and I in him,
The same bringeth forth much fruit:
For without Me ye can do nothing." –John 15:5

"All is in Christ, by the Holy Spirit,
For the glory of God. All else is
Nothing." –Joseph Carroll

Our new church location was only 50 miles south of the seminary, so it wasn't a complicated move. We had very little and so a couple pickup trucks and our car did the job. The parsonage was lovely, and DiAnne soon decorated and made it home. Even though I was somewhat familiar with the facilities, the deacons took me on an orientation walk to share details. **I still remember the words in my head as we walked around – "I will do well at this."** As I mentioned early on, **I had developed the wicked way of self-sufficiency, and I was totally oblivious to my problem. I actually thought it was a good thing. God would soon show me a different way.** I totally relate to David when he wrote, "Search me, O God, and know my heart; try me, and know my thoughts; and see if there be any wicked way in me, and lead me in the way everlasting." (Psalm 139:23, 24). The Lord was faithful to answer David's prayer on my behalf because I didn't even know I had a problem.

In those days, our genre of churches promoted the idea that church growth was all about big days, hard work, and hard preaching. There was also a lot of competition between the churches over attendance and baptisms. Everyone operated on their own level of awareness, so my thinking was:

1. If it's hard work – a German farmer can handle it.
2. If it's competition – an athletic competitor can handle it.
3. If it's hard preaching – I have trained for this. I will do well.
4. If it's big days – I will be fun and creative.

Let me pause here and say, it brings pain and grief to me now as I write this reflecting on my inner self. But this was all I knew. At the same time, I want to extend grace to all who read this that there is nothing intrinsically wrong with these tools if they are God-ordained for your situation. No guilt is intended here – only a heart that needed to learn a better way.

We hit the ground running. On the first Wednesday night after a hard message, Ruth was saved. She was our first fruits. Then we had "picture" day. I was on the parking lot snapping pictures with my Polaroid camera as families got out of the car. Then we had baby day and so on. Working hard was no problem. Arising every weekday morning at 5:30, I was live on the radio at 6:05, I had a goal to make 50 visits a week while overseeing administrative duties and studying for preaching. I often arrived home at 10 p.m.

DiAnne, who was now pregnant with our third child, Jewel, asked me one day, "Have you noticed how Jason laughs and plays with Bo (a man in our church) after the services?" I actually had seen my son enjoying the ride on Bo's shoulders. Her question gave me pause,but there was no significant change. **Hard work and sacrifice was my way.** One severe blow to our marriage was when I personally borrowed money from the bank in order to give to a church building project. When the payment stubs came in the mail, it hurt her deeply. She had sacrificed and lived on a shoestring budget through college and seminary and was looking for better financial footing for us and the children. With a third baby on the way, this brought even further insecurity. All of this was in keeping with my learned paradigm

H̄ard work and sacrifice was my way.

of ministry; ministry happens when we work hard, promote excitedly, and preach interestingly. All in all we seemed to be doing well. Attendance grew, we were becoming family, and we called Dave to be pastor of music and youth. He was a dear servant. He and I are best friends yet today. He fell in love with our secretary, Connie, and I married them. Connie was in my original youth group. Several came to know the Lord. We even started proceedings to expand our K-5 program to a full-fledged Christian school. But inwardly, I was dying. **The combination of exhaustion, ignorance, constant responsibility, and mild turbulence amongst the leaders rendered me powerless, and I crashed and burned.** I found myself crippled with worry, fear, and depression. Often I reflected on how cocky I was in seminary when others reported church troubles. I thought "Bless God that won't happen to me." I thought I was strong.

I also struggled with lustful thinking, which I know is common for men, but I was deeply convicted and didn't know what to do about it. It's difficult to preach hard against sin when you yourself have no answers for those you are just beating up with your words. Finally, I wasn't sure if we were experiencing lasting fruit or just a swelling crowd. I was so defeated by all of this that I would curl up on the floor in my jean jacket, listen to Christian music for comfort, play possum, and long for the farm. There were times when church members would come, I would stay in that position, my wife would "cover" for me, and they would step over me and enjoy their visit with her. Needless to say, I was not doing well at this. Something had to change, but what?

Around that same time, our youth under Dave's leadership had done some door-to-door visitation and met an older lady named Sarah. They came back with excitement, telling us about her humor and spiritual insights. She visited our church and soon became dear friends with my wife. She developed a mom-mentor relationship with DiAnne. As we grew closer to her, she began to share books, articles, and tapes with us. She sensed that we had good hearts but did

Soon I would be learning that the primary importance was not how I came across to an audience but rather how He came across through me.

know not the way of the Vine. She was always respectful and pleasant, never chiding me because of my ignorance. She was a great help to my wife as she chuckled and prayed over our problems, always ending the conversation with a nugget she had read. I admired her ability to give wisdom without ridicule or dogmatism. This was a grace I wanted to emulate.

During this time, Sarah gave us a tape by Joseph Carroll and suggested that it might be a blessing. One day as I was traveling to have lunch with one of our deacons, I popped it in. Woven into the message on "How to Worship Jesus Christ," Mr. Carroll related an illustration about a defeated missionary that he once counseled. When he described the condition of the missionary, he could just as well been describing me. At that moment, the Holy Spirit captured my full attention. I was broken, desperate, and hungry. If something didn't change, I would be out of the ministry and who knows after that. Here's what he said to the missionary – as if speaking directly to me.

"Jesus is your <u>Savior</u>. That's what He did <u>for</u> us. Romans 5:8 says, 'But God commendeth His love toward us, in that, while we were yet sinners, Christ died for us.'" I knew this.

"Jesus is our <u>sanctification</u>. That's what He does <u>in</u> us. I Corinthians 1:30 (says) 'But of Him are ye in Christ Jesus, who of God is made unto us wisdom, and righteousness, and sanctification, and redemption'." I had never seen this but when I heard it that day, a light came on and offered hope for my purity.

"Jesus is our <u>service</u>. That's what He does <u>through</u> us. John 15:5 says 'I am the Vine, ye are the branches; He that abideth in Me, and I in him, the same bringeth forth much fruit; for without Me ye can do nothing'." Another light came on. This was my hope for lasting fruit. Before it was all about my performance in the pulpit. **Soon I would be learning that the primary importance was not how I came across to an audience but rather how He came across through me.**

"Jesus is our Shepherd. That's what He does <u>with</u> us. Psalm 23:1 says 'The Lord is my Shepherd, I shall not want.'" This addressed my battle with worry and fear. At the end of this story he said, "In the same way that you let Jesus be your Savior by faith, you need to let Him be your life by faith – your sanctification, your service and your Shepherd."

As Mr. Carroll was finishing his remarks, my heart was pounding, my spirit was leaping, and my tears were flowing. **I had found my answer right where it needed to be – in Jesus.**

About that time, I pulled into the McDonald's near Marietta, Georgia, to meet my friend. He wasn't there yet – I was glad because it gave me time to pray. Stepping out of my car, I bowed my head on top of that '67 Pontiac and prayed something like this: "Lord, in the same way I received You by faith to be my Savior, I now believe you as my sanctification, my service, and my Shepherd. Thank You. I love You."

My life and ministry was changed that day. Christ in me would be my new starting point. I began to look at all ministry and preaching differently. There would be a lot to learn. My late wife would tell you, as she told many audiences, "I got a new husband that day, our kids got a new father, and our church got a new pastor." **The life of the Vine was now real in the soul of the preacher.**

9
Back to the Bible

"One thing I have desired of the Lord,
That will I seek after; that I may dwell
In the house of the Lord all the days of
My life, to behold the beauty of the Lord,
And to enquire in His temple." –Psalm 27:4

"Every successful man I have ever met
Had come at some time under the
dominating power of a great truth." –Bob Jones Sr.

What happened to me next is vital to this story. Without this piece of the puzzle, everything experiential will evaporate in the hot sun of daily living and the diversity of trials life may bring. Don't miss this part!

Being thrilled with what God had shown me about Jesus being my life, I went everywhere telling my story. The very day I arrived home from Marietta and walked in the church building, I saw Dave praying alone at the altar. As we talked quietly, he spoke of his hunger for reality, too, so I shared my experience. At dinner I shared with DiAnne and the kids, who were 5, 3 and 1 at the time; I was bubbling over. I began formulating messages to try to relate with our congregation what God was doing. God had given me a new victory, freedom, hope, and joy. I felt confident and still do feel that this message of Christ in you and through you and with you is the answer for everything. I told my brother pastors, my former classmates, my parents, my wife's parents. I read everything

I could find on this idea. Needless to say, I was enjoying this new reality and longed for definition and looked for those who would understand and rejoice with me.

The response to my exuberance was varied. Some smiled courteously as if I were a grandma talking on about her twenty-first grandchild; others seemed blank. There were a few who eagerly related and queried for more dialogue. They were very encouraging. Some quickly labeled it as a common case of preacher burn-out. One strong ministry leader told me straight up that I should stop talking about it because he felt I was on the verge of doctrinal imbalance. I didn't think so, but his advice made me realize that I didn't have a handle – at least in accurately communicating my newly found treasure. I continued to ponder and enjoy.

This went on for a period of two years, and to my surprise and chagrin, I CRASHED and BURNED again! I was devastated, and this time doubly confused because I thought I had found the answer in Jesus. Like Peter I thought, "Where can I go? Jesus had the Words of Eternal Life," (John 6:68). Maybe my feelings could be likened to how the disciples felt on the road to Emmaus after the resurrection and missing body of Jesus; I was very sad.

During that time, I received in the mail an envelope which contained a small booklet. It was green and had Galatians 2:20 on the front. It had no return address and no note. To this day, I don't know who sent it. Isn't that just like God? I actually opened the envelope and read the booklet in the car while my wife went into the grocery store. These details are only given because I want you to know my awareness of the moment. God was about to rescue His struggling son. As I read the book, the author who I don't remember, actually chronicled his journey with Jesus, and it paralleled mine identically. It's like I was reading my own autobiography, including the Second Depression! As I searchingly read on, the writer told of how this second crash for him was meant by God to turn him back to the written Word of God and prevent a fall into the error of living on experience or feelings, both of which can be deceptive and fickle.

That was it! God had done it again. He had made real the next lesson. **I was to find the reality of the living Word, Jesus, through the objective truth of the written Word.** God wanted me to always

I was to find the reality of the living Word (Jesus) through the objective truth of the written Word.

build my life and ministry on the more sure prophecy of the Word. The enlightenment of the Ephesians gives clear Scriptural instructions for the truth (Eph. 1:15-23). I began right then to become extremely intentional with my meeting time with God in the word. Objective truth (logos) and subjective reality (rhema) became the balance and best of both worlds. The Bible became my final authority, my absolute truth, my instructions for living, and my meeting place with God. I can dwell in His presence, behold His beauty, and ask Him questions while He changes me. "But we all, with open face beholding as in a glass the glory of the Lord, are changed into the same image from glory to glory, even as by the Spirit of the Lord" (II Cor. 3:18). In a few years, God would visit us with a heaven-sent revival, and this lesson would be key to preserving what He would do.

Feeling – Faith – Fact

Three men were walking on a wall,
Feeling, Faith and Fact,
When Feeling took an awful fall,
And Faith was taken back.
So close was Faith to Feeling.
He stumbled and fell, too,
But Fact remained and pulled Faith up,
And he brought Feeling, too.

10
Issues or Jesus

*"For I determined not to know
anything among you, save Jesus
Christ, and Him crucified"*
                    –I Corinthians 2:2

"Nothing is so deadening to the
divine as an habitual dealing
with the outsides of holy things."
                    –George MacDonald

We were approaching the 4-year mark in our first church when I received a surprise call from Dr. Gerry Benn, who was one of my professors in seminary. He was a Canadian and was being called to go back to his home country and start a seminary. He shared his calling and then asked if I would pray about coming to take the pastorate of the church he had started just 10 years prior. I was honored by his faith in me as a former student, thrilled at the possibilities, but scared by the academia in the church and the city. This was a church with credentials started by a man with credentials located at the foothills of the school that gave the credentials. I knew that I was still a novice and very ignorant but was learning that Jesus was my life. While praying about this, the Lord showed me Mark 10:32.

"And they were in the way going up to Jerusalem; and Jesus went before them: and they were amazed; and as they followed, they were afraid." That verse described perfectly how I felt about this. I was following Jesus back to the main city. I was amazed and afraid. So we said yes.

The friends in our first church saw the hand of God in this and sent us off graciously. We still love and remember them. Not long ago, I spoke back in that area, and many of them came. I will always remember them as the saints who loved a scared young preacher into the right direction. They were like that dear lady in Jesus's day "who had suffered many things" at the hands of the physicians. In their case, they had suffered at the hands of many poor sermons! Her plight lasted 12 long years. Fortunately, theirs only lasted four.

The new church was more than wonderful. A great foundation had been laid. They were humble, loving, young, and smart. They were hard-working people with a servant spirit. It was 1976. I had just turned 30, and our nation turned 200. We had an exciting Christian school with a Bible-based, Christ-centered curriculum. Our congregation was made up of students, college graduates, seminary graduates, doctors, lawyers, other professional people, veteran servants of God, common laborers, and many new babes in Christ. We worshiped as one, sang with gusto, studied the Word, and loved each other. Sadly, because of the weak leadership of their new pastor, something would creep in that would scatter this delightful flock – something I deeply regret to this day. It was my entire fault. To talk of this now brings me more pain than it did then. Perhaps this discussion will stop another young shepherd from making the same mistake.

Over the course of the first 18 months, we grew numerically. It was healthy growth mixing town folks, students, and new converts. We were a transient congregation, so we gained about 200 and lost 100 (for good reason). Our Christian school was growing. We had a gifted and handsome young teaching staff – a good mix of men and women. But in varied, inconspicuous ways, we were becoming an "issue-oriented" church.

We were a young church with energy for debate. We had students who were forming their convictions and loved to weigh all the pros and cons. We had academia who made their living with teaching and learning a new thing. We had legalists who had to defend their loyalty to the party line. We even entered into a class

There is no life in anything if it is detached from the Vine no matter how noble the cause.

action lawsuit with other churches against the United States government and then Secretary of Labor, Ray Marshall, on the principle that Christ was the Head of the church and should not be taxed by the State. This was a conviction for us, and I was a pastor who wanted to please everybody, know all the answers, and do the most right thing.

Tragically, quietly, and subtly – Jesus went on the back burner, and good issues took center-stage. I let good-hearted, well-intentioned, intelligent people replace Jesus with subtle substitutions. We became a "Mars Hill" where … "the Athenians and the strangers who were there spent their time in nothing else, but either to tell, or to hear some new thing" (Acts 17:21).

If you were to ask me at the time, I would have been convinced that Jesus was the main focus. **Philosophically, we were true to Scripture, but practically, the time, the light, and the heat was spent on secondary issues.** Like the church at Ephesus (Revelation 2:1-7), we couldn't bear those who were evil; we tested false teachers; we persevered; we were patient and labored for Jesus with vigor, but we were gradually drifting from our first love. While we were diligently taking a stand, we were losing power, compassion, joy, and outreach. The brush fires gave us no rest – discernment turned to judgment, and I ran out of grace for it all. One brother suggested that I was the problem and that the church could not be what it ought to be with me at the helm. He was a good man who had given much counsel to the church body. His suggestion, coupled with my exhaustion, led to my resignation the next day. I resigned in faith with no place to go. Interestingly, my wife (now with four little ones) was okay with it. I resigned on a Wednesday, and the next day was Thanksgiving 1980. That next morning, I was alone reading the Word, and God gave me Psalm 37:23, "The steps of a good man are ordained by the Lord; and He delighteth in his way." The Lord assured me that He delighted in my way and what would happen next would prove it.

Leaving this wonderful church in disarray because of my weak leadership has written on my heart the following valuable lessons.

1. A church can be doing everything right and still be in trouble with Jesus.
2. Leaving our first love for Jesus is the first place where churches go wrong.
3. Never let anything but the person and work of Jesus take center stage in a ministry. Good and very good can surely be the enemy of the best. I have learned to call these subtle substitutes for Jesus.

There is no life in anything if it is detached from the Vine, no matter how noble the cause.

11
Homesick or God's Call

*"See, I have this day set thee
Over the nations and over the
kingdoms, to root out, and to
Pull down, and to destroy, and
To throw down, to build, and
To plant".* –Jeremiah 1:10

"A man of God in the will of
God is immortal until His work
Is done." –David Jeremiah

Leaving a ministry with no place to go was a bold step of faith for us. We were a young family with four children age 11 and under. As I said earlier, DiAnne seemed to be at peace with my decision. We agreed that I could get a job and then wait on the Lord's placement. What happened next was a providential miracle of God.

The Monday after my resignation, the deacons met to discuss the situation. After their meeting, one of them called me and said, "We don't want you to leave; would you please reconsider? We love you and want you to stay. We believe we can work things out." I thought for a second. Perhaps I was hasty. Maybe I was just tired and needed to rest but not resign. So I said, "Okay, let me pray about it, and we can talk Wednesday after prayer meeting." He agreed.

Let me interject here that from the time I had trusted Jesus, I had a longing to go back to my home area and minister to my family and community. It never left. It grew. In June of 1980, the desire was so strong that I went to our downstairs bedroom, laid on my face before the Lord, and cried out, "Lord, please move me or change me." Both my wife and I needed to know if this burden was from the Lord or just homesickness. She had seen me be a big baby about this. God would soon show us.

After the deacon call on Monday evening, I started my Tuesday with a time in the Word and prayer. In my normal routine, I was just waiting and rationalizing that probably I had made a mistake. Early afternoon the phone rang in my office, and it was a man from the Calvary Baptist Church of Danville, Illinois – 8 miles north of my hometown. He said, "Pastor Humrichous, our pastor recently resigned, and we wondered if you would consider coming to be our pastor?" The discussion of this moment still gives me a pause with chills. **This was God's impeccable sovereign timing for a guy who wasn't sure about desires or choices. My precious Father was ordering my steps.**

I need to note here that this was the third time this church had invited us to come. In the summer of 1968, between my junior and senior year in college, I had filled the pulpit there in the absence of a pastor. They invited me to consider being their pastor, but knowing my immaturity and need to finish college, I said no – wrong timing. Ten years later, after being at the Chattanooga church for less than 2 years, another representative came from Calvary with the same invitation. Again, I didn't think it ethically right to leave a church after such a short time. Six months after I turned the second offer down, my dear father died suddenly on December 22nd. He was 55. It was Christmas. This left my mother and my only brother with a large farming enterprise. Did I miss God's opportunity to be home with them? This third invitation was God's perfect timing. My wife was convinced of God's call. How thankful I was for her sake. She had gone through much with me and having her be sure of this call and bold move would free her up and give her the security of knowing this was of God, not just my emotions. On Wednesday after prayer meeting, I shared my phone call with them, and they all agreed that

This was God's impeccable sovereign timing for a guy who wasn't sure about desires or choices. My precious Father was ordering my steps.

this was the hand of God. After 30 days, they sent us off with their blessings. We burned no bridges. I still get gracious notes from some of them.

We had one more emotional obstacle. It was DiAnne's loving, mentoring relationship with Sarah Merry. She said, "I believe this is of the Lord, but I don't want to leave Sarah." Sarah meant the world to us. She introduced us to new truth in love. She believed God with us. She taught us to choose joy in times of difficult obedience. She was my wife's best friend outside of her family. God worked.

Sarah always was strong in spirit but frail in body. As we were preparing to move, Sarah became ill and was taken to the hospital for routine tests. While there, her son carefully attending to her, she choked on water and died. Sarah was gone. Her funeral was a simple graveside service. Her grave was almost completely obscure when we visited it just before our move. We both knew that God had used this saint to do His work in our lives and then moved her home to glory.

Within 4 years, her influence and the seeds she had sown would bear much fruit when again we would find ourselves thrust into a new arena of God's heart for His church.

12
Death to Self

"Knowing this, that our old man is crucified with Him, that the body of sin might be destroyed, that henceforth we should not serve sin." –Romans 6:6

"No one will reach their full potential in Christ until they effectively deal with their self-life."   –jch

There is one more piece of truth we must include before we leave this section of the book. It is the subject of death to the self-life.

The great truth of "death to self" had been introduced to me in bits and pieces. Occasionally, I would have spiritual glimpses of it, but the reality of its power in my life did not grip me until I embraced by faith my position and identification with Christ in His death, burial and resurrection – according to the clear statement of Scripture.

"Know ye not, that so many of us as were baptized into Jesus Christ were baptized into His death? Therefore we are buried with Him by baptism into death: that like as Christ was raised up from the dead by the glory of the Father, even so we also should walk in newness of life." –Romans 6:3, 4

"Likewise reckon ye also yourselves to be dead indeed unto sin, but alive unto God through Jesus Christ our Lord." –Romans 6:11

"I am crucified with Christ; nevertheless I live; yet not I, but Christ liveth in me; and the life which I now live in the flesh I live by the faith of the Son of God, who loved me, and gave Himself for me."
–Galatians 2:20

"But God forbid that I should glory save in the cross of our Lord Jesus Christ, by whom the world is crucified unto me, and I unto the world."
–Galatians 6:14

Books have been written on this subject, and I have read many of them. The real break-through in my understanding, however, was when I got serious with one verse – Romans 6:6. There I saw that my old man was crucified with Jesus. He had been crucified for me, and I had been crucified with Him. The body of sin/flesh could now be rendered powerless, and I did not have to serve the wicked empire of sin. I was now free to choose. I understood for the first time that the cross not only paid for the penalty of sin, but it delivers from the power of the sin nature and establishes the posture of the believer's attitude. We must learn to minister with the attitude of the cross. **The life of the Vine flows richly when the servant of God is keenly aware that "in my flesh dwelleth no good thing"** (Romans 7:18).

To have a sensitive, easily offended pastor is a miserable plight for any congregation.

In his book *"The Cross and Christian Ministry"*, D.A. Carson says, "The cross not only establishes <u>what</u> we are to preach, but <u>how</u> we are to preach." We should neither be arrogant or touchy. The people we serve should not be afraid of us. Nor should we have to be coddled by them. **To have a sensitive, easily offended pastor is a miserable plight for any congregation.**

Through appropriating my death with Christ and by taking hurtful things to the cross, I wanted to be in the process of becoming unoffendable

Jesus won a lion-like victory through a lamb-like means.

except in matters that offended the gospel of Christ or His sheep. A verse that has been a great encouragement in this direction is Psalm 119:165, "Great peace have they which love thy law; and nothing shall offend them." **Words of praise must not swell our heads, and words of criticism must not embitter our hearts.** Those who are dead to self and filled with the Spirit are easy to live with. Fighting good battles with the bad fleshy weapons only causes more harm. In his very excellent book *"The Crucified King"*, Dr. Jeremy Treat says, "Jesus won a lion-like victory through a lamb-like means." (Rev. 5:5, 6; Phil. 2:1-8). **In ministry lions and lambs lay down together.**

A. **How can we recognize self-life? Here are some common characteristics:**
   • Spirit of pride – Exalted feelings in view of your success or position (could also be inferior feelings or self-pity if we fail)
   • Love of human praise – Fondness to be noticed; drawing attention to self
   • Stirring of anger or impatience – Touchy; sensitive spirit; dislikes being contradicted
   • Self-will – A stubborn, unteachable spirit; unyielded; headstrong
   • Carnal fear – Man-fearing spirit
   • Jealous disposition – Unpleasant sensation in view of the great prosperity and success of another
   • Dishonest, deceitful disposition – Evading and covering the truth
   • Unbelief –Lack of faith and trust in God
   • Sensual Spirit –Satisfying legitimate passion in illegitimate ways

When you are forgotten or neglected, or purposely set at naught, and you don't sting and hurt with the insult or the oversight, but your heart is happy, being counted worthy to suffer for Christ, *THAT IS DYING TO SELF.*

When your good is evil spoken of, when your wishes are crossed, your advice disregarded, your opinions ridiculed, and you refuse to let anger rise in your heart, or even defend yourself, but take it all in patience, loving silence, *THAT IS DYING TO SELF.*

When you lovingly and patiently bear any disorder, any irregularity and unpunctuality, or any annoyance; when you stand face to face with waste, folly, extravagance, spiritual insensibility, and endure it as Jesus endured it, *THAT IS DYING TO SELF.*

When you never care to refer to yourself in conversation, or to record your own good works, or itch after commendation, when you can truly love to be unknown, *THAT IS DYING TO SELF.*

When you are content with any food, any offering, any raiment, any climate, any society, any solitude, any interruption by the will of God, *THAT IS DYING TO SELF.*

When you can see your brother prosper and have his needs met, and can honestly rejoice with him in spirit and feel no envy or question God, while your own needs are far greater and in desperate circumstances, *THAT IS DYING TO SELF.*

When you can receive correction and reproof from one of less stature than yourself, and you can humbly submit inwardly as well as outwardly, finding no rebellion or resentment rising up within your heart, *THAT IS DYING TO SELF.*

–Author Unknown

Attitudes are more often caught than taught. It's confusing to our sheep if they hear the message of Christ but see the message of flesh. This also holds true for our families, especially our wives and children. Jesus said it best. "Verily, verily, I say unto you, except a corn of wheat fall into the ground and die, it abideth alone; but if it dies, it bringeth forth much fruit" (John 12:24). No servant of God hopes to abide alone.

Conclusion to Section #1

At this stage in the journey, I was 34 and had been a Christian for 15 years. In God's great faithfulness, He had moved me to the full reality that salvation was not a plan but rather a person. I hope that sounds profoundly simple yet powerful to you. It postures us to be in love with the One who is worthy of our full affection. The "Plan" became flesh and dwelt among us. We could then behold His glory.

By faith Jesus had become my salvation, my sufficiency, and my satisfaction. He was very real to me now. I was resolved to keep Him center stage in my life and ministry. We were headed back to my beloved homeland to minister. The truths of this section had been engrafted in my soul. We would soon meet others who also understood the life of the Vine in the soul of the preacher. It was becoming what John Piper describes as "Being totally satisfied with all that God wants to become to us through Christ," and it was offering unspeakable joy – and still is.

SECTION TWO

*The Life of the Vine
in the Heart of Revival*

13

A New Resolve

"Come unto Me, all ye that labour and are heavy laden,
And I will give you rest. Take My yoke upon you, and
learn of Me; for I am meek and lowly in heart: and ye
shall find rest unto your souls. For My yoke is easy, and
My burden is light." –Matthew 11:28-30

"Everyone operates at their own level of awareness."
–Unknown

We arrived at our new church, Calvary Baptist Church of Danville, Illinois, in January of 1981. My heart was so full. A clear call from God, a new level of awareness about Jesus, a new resolve about leadership, and the security of my wife about the move set me ready for service. The church was excited because they also saw the hand of God during the transition. We were 15 miles from the farm where my now widowed mother lived. I could help her. I could help my brother on the farm. I could work at my old Bible camp during the summer, and I was on the mission field close to many schoolmates who needed Jesus. God had brought us back full and ready to serve.

The church itself had been troubled. One gentleman in the church said, "If it doesn't work this time, we are going to close the doors." He was exaggerating because of the emotional exhaustion. A local pastor said, "Joe won't last 6 months." His statement was based on the track record of those shepherds before me. All I knew was God had called us there, and I was excited to preach this new reality of Jesus to them. I had no agenda or strategy other than Christ Himself. On the first Sunday, when I went to the platform and DiAnne went to the piano, we both noticed

We began to experience the worthlessness of fallow ground.

that the first 10 rows were empty! This seating posture let us know that Jesus needed to show up. They had learned the hard realities of the organized church but were missing the healing, life-giving realities of Jesus. So we began preaching the sufficiency of the Scriptures and the sufficiency of Christ, and the Lord began to heal us and grow us. The Head (Jesus) began nourishing the body, knitting us together, and increasing us with the increase of God (Col. 2:19). It was glorious to watch. With spiritual health and wellness came other physical blessings like finances, infrastructure, synergy, and outreach. This went on for about two and a half years.

At that point, the tests began to come. God was faithful to apply pressure in various ways so that real needs in lives would surface. God has a way of making things "manifest" (I Cor. 11:19) in order to prove the faithful. We did not tank, but we did plateau and settle some. Those who were riding the wave, but not entering in, began to look at attendance and offerings, and the undercurrent of murmuring began. There was no overt rebellion, and most were gracious to me, but we began to experience the worthlessness of fallow ground, which then gives way to blame shifting and excuses for sin, unbelief, and lack of surrender to the Lordship of Christ. This went on for a year and a half. My personal faith in the joy and reality of Christ was never shaken. By this time, there was a core who embraced this same reality, but we seemed impotent in affecting the needed breakthrough.

My faith in Jesus was strong, and my home was joyful, but I was at my wits end in knowing how to communicate and lead this congregation to higher ground.

Our home was 176 steps from the church building. I was usually the last one to leave the building, so many of my walks home often became a celebration or reflection of the service we just had. One day as I walked, I simply asked the Lord, "Am I going to have to leave another independent, fundamental, Bible believing, Baptist Church without them entering into the reality of who You are?" He would soon answer my question.

14
Life Action
The Covington/Danville Revival
(February-March 1985)

"For thus saith the high and lofty One that inhabiteth eternity;
Whose name is Holy: I dwell in the high and holy place, with Him also that is of a contrite and humble spirit, to revive the Spirit of the humble, and to revive the heart of the contrite Ones." –Isaiah 57:15

"You must fall on the Rock and be broken or the Rock will fall
On you and crush you." –(A call to brokenness
and repentance based
on Matthew 21:44)

During the very time I was questioning how to lead our church into the reality of Christ, unbeknown to me, Dr. Gregg Curtis and the First Baptist Church of Covington, Indiana, were praying for revival. Covington was directly east of us 13 miles. They were led to schedule Life Action Revival Ministries from Niles, Michigan for a two-week meeting.

Realizing the varied thoughts about the subject of revival, please trust my integrity in reporting accurately about the seven-and-a-half weeks in which God worked. I will proceed with caution knowing that there are those off and on the scene who do not look favorably on those days. I am writing this chapter exactly 30 years later. I also know that the landscape of the church has changed with the influx of mega-churches and emphasis on "seeker sensitivity." From that there is a growth of reform theology returning us to the power of the gospel as a response to easy believism and a consumer mentality. Revivalists even approach this subject differently. My point in this chapter is to illustrate how God used this sovereign, unplanned visitation to move me down the road of understanding and to bless many others with the reality of Christ through repentance. So relax. I will be careful.

The full report of these meetings is written up in the August 1985 edition of *The Spirit of Revival* magazine by Dr. Gregg Curtis. I will reference him as well as insert my own experience.

I resisted attending the meetings at first thinking that it was mostly a musical presentation, some choreography, and some preaching. Our assistant pastor asked me if we were going to attend the Covington meeting, and I responded, "No." He asked, "Why?," and I said, "We don't need a song and dance routine; we need reality in Jesus." Reports started coming and kept coming about changed lives. First Baptist had a radio station, so they put testimonies from the meetings on the air, and I would hear them as I traveled in my car. I liked the spirit of the leader Del Fehsenfeld II. So I took a friend, and we went on Thursday night during the second week. God was changing lives, and their testimonies were moving. After the service, someone introduced me to Del, and in a very short time, God gave me a dear brother in Del, who traveled with a large family of believers who had a growing understanding of revival and would help me interpret and apply the principles of personal revival which had changed my life 11 years before. During this seven-week period, I was introduced to a whole new world of people who knew what I needed to learn. God gave me a revival family.

The meeting stayed in First Baptist for four weeks then moved 13 miles west to our church and continued another three-and-a-half weeks. We were very blessed. God gave us exactly what we needed.

My joy was beyond description. Here are some things I learned during those weeks.

1. Sometimes our hearts need to be plowed and not every preacher is gifted that way. Both Jeremiah (4:3) and Hosea (10:12) tell us to break up our fallow ground and seek the Lord. Dr. Curtis said, "Each night the Holy Spirit stuck the plow in a little deeper. Although plowing is painful, it is a vital part of the whole process of revival. If there is not first a breaking of hard or resistant hearts, then planting seeds of truth will do no good." This idea was new to me and I have tried to apply this truth in ministry ever since.

2. Repentance transforms prayer, and prayer transforms repentance. Curtis says, "Challenged by a vision of what God could do if we sought Him with all our hearts, our church was transformed into a house of prayer." We prayed before, during, and after the meetings. We prayed in the auditorium and in the prayer room. We prayed all night at times. Prayer was not forced or boring. We wanted to be together in prayer.

3. Rightness with God leads to rightness with man. Curtis said, "People began to realize that it was impossible to be right with God and not be right with one another. Barriers of guilt, selfishness, and pride were torn down between God's people." On the first night I went, many were apologizing publicly for their malice.

4. Personal testimonies are used by God to cross-pollinate other believers with grace to respond favorably to God. For the first time, I saw the powerful influence of the witness of changed lives. Conviction and repentance seemed to spread from one to another without preaching.

5. The grace that comes through humility, honesty, and wholeness affects our physical energy. The services were long, the nights were late, but we had strength and loved it. We also gained a new boldness to share Christ with others.

Only the Lord knows the full effects of these weeks. I am sensing the results to be deep and wide. Some have fallen away. Some never followed through. There is a large nucleus of us, however, who will never be the same and never forget what we learned during those days. The themes of repentance of sin, death to self, and the filling of the Spirit were deeply embedded in our lives.

As a pastor-teacher, I believed this move of God would have to be followed up in order for us to be good stewards of what He had done. At this point, now 30 years ago, I became a student of the stewardship of God's reviving. Del would advise me of our next step, and I would move forward with my new revival family.

15
The Sutera Revival
(October 1987)

*"Take heed therefore unto yourselves, and to all the flock,
Over which the Holy Ghost hath made you overseers, to
feed the church of God, which He hath purchased with
His own blood." –Acts 20:28*

"When Moses said, 'I can't,' God said 'I AM'."
–Les Ollila

During the last few days of the Covington meeting and throughout the days in our church, Del and I had some time to develop a relationship strategic to what God was doing during this time. Even though he was younger, he became my mentor in revival matters. Through his life, I learned to answer personal questions like, "Do I find you praying?" and "Joe, what is God doing in your life today?" I watched him and his wife, Judy, press on even during the miscarriage of their baby. I learned the difference between seeking God's face and seeking God's hand. I observed Del remain open for counsel from critics when the ministry team came under fire. His humility and teachable spirit was attractive to me. As the meetings came to a close, I knew that we would need his wisdom in moving forward as stewards of what God had done. So I asked, "Where should we go from here?" His immediate response was to recommend a revival team associated with the Canadian Revival Fellowship in Regina, Saskatchewan, Canada.

The names of the team leaders were Ralph and Lou Sutera, who actually lived in Mansfield, Ohio, at the time. Del said, "These men will make these difficult revival truths clear and will present them in a pleasant, joyful manner which will be received by all ages" and then gave me their contact information. I would find that everything he said about them was true – plus much more. We contacted the Suteras, and a three-and-a half-week meeting was scheduled for October 1987, which gave us two-and-a-half years to prepare.

Ralph and Lou were born on April 27, 1932, in Brooklyn, New York. Their parents were staunch Italian Roman Catholics. Through a series of illnesses, God brought them to faith in Christ alone and at the age of eight, the twins were converted. At age 14, they entered Bob Jones Academy and continued their education at Bob Jones University, graduating cum laude in 1953.

After 18 years of crusade ministry, the Suteras came to the Ebenezer Baptist Church in Saskatoon, Saskatchewan, Canada – October 13, 1971. That meeting became Canada's first national revival. In his book *Flames of Freedom*, Dr. Erwin Lutzer said, "A 12-day crusade in a small Baptist church had stretched to seven weeks. The evangelical churches of the city had been shaken by the persistent work of the Holy Spirit." From this movement which went south to the U.S. and around the world, the Canadian Revival Fellowship was formed. These revival veterans and their team were now scheduled for our church!

Ralph advised us to prepare far in advance. He suggested we have no outside speakers except our own missionaries and those who had been changed in revival and were willing to share their testimonies. That we did. People from within our church, people from the life action meeting in other churches, and people from around the country that Ralph and Lou would recommend. We learned so much from them. I learned the difference between good men and Spirit-filled men. Prayer meetings began about a year in advance. We even began to collect offerings ahead of time in lieu of a longer meeting and the support of the team families.

Our congregation was well vested in the effort in many different ways.

God even gave good weather that fall for an early harvest so our many farm families could give their undivided attention to the meetings. Almost everyone was waiting in anticipation for the curtain to rise and for God to show up.

When the team arrived, they were all 50+, which contrasted with Life Action, who were 18-40. This was good for our congregation because it witnessed to our mature audience that revival was not just an emotional youth movement but was a reality to seasoned, mature saints as well. This really helped me as a leader keep our most influential veterans on board. God used this one factor to win over some who were skeptical.

Lou preached on Sunday morning, announcing with great vigor the beginning of the revival effort on Monday evening! He said, "Now, tomorrow night, we will begin our revival, and I'm going to speak on 'Where does revival begin?' Don't miss it." As I listened to his promotion, I was bummed for two reasons. (1) I thought this effort should begin on Sunday morning. Why is he saying Monday night? (2) I just knew he was going to say that revival should begin in us – you know the old proverbial, "Draw a circle and get in it, and let revival begin in your circle." Quite frankly, I didn't want anything else to begin with me!

Monday night came, and Lou began. "Now tonight I'm going to tell you where revival begins; I'm sure you all want to know." I was braced. "Okay, here it is. **A revival that begins in the <u>character of God</u> is as a river ever widening and deepening until it falls into the expanse of God's great eternity. Ladies and gentlemen, a revival must begin in the character of God!**"

For me, this moment was the defining moment for the meeting, and it has remained a defining statement for my life

A revival that begins in the character of God is as a river ever widening and deepening until it falls into the expanse of God's great eternity.

and ministry. Lou spoke for 90 minutes from Romans Chapter 1 on the threefold sin of society. I sensed that God engulfed us with Himself that night, and our perspective of real revival was set in place for the duration of the meeting. Most of the response came from the faithful in our congregation who hungered for God, and they began to lead the way for others.

The three-and-a-half weeks went as planned with a healthy love and receptivity from the entire congregation. Not everyone came to everything, but there were no critical repercussions anywhere. The meetings trailed off in attendance toward the end, which I learned later was common to the strategy of the Suteras. In fact, their approach was to begin with a "bang" and "big God" truths. As they saw the response to go to the prayer room slow down, they moved to more of a teaching mode in order to ground those who had made life-changing decisions. This worked well. The dam of the "river of revival" had been broken, and we were left with a refreshing stream of God's Spirit flowing through the pasture where our sheep would water. We were not panicky in how we would keep anything going. It was very helpful to me as the under shepherd.

The Sutera meeting deepened us in the truths we had previously heard. It broadened us in the number of people who entered in. It defined terms and concepts for more understanding. One of the giant things I learned was the difference between objective truth and subjective reality. It allowed me to be able to teach people how Jesus could be real to our souls while not sacrificing the objective truth of God's Word. We must never lose the foundation of Scripture while seeking an experiential relationship with Jesus. We can have both. We learned that revival must "come down" and not be "drummed up." We learned how to allow the Holy Spirit to convince us of sin, righteousness, and judgment. **Even attempting to confess and repent in the flesh can prove to be futile or even fatal to our walk.**

Above all things, through Ralph and Lou, we were given a worldwide network of people from many walks of life who understood the way of God's Spirit. They also offered many ways for me and others from our congregation to get involved by sharing our testimonies. They prayed over my wife and me and our children. They ate in our home, made friends with our people, and seemed to rejoice with every little victory. We adopted them as our life-long mentors, and their follow-up connection set us on a course that continues to flourish to this day. The joyous realities would soon be even more focused.

Addendum To Suteras (December 1987)

After our meeting with the Suteras, someone, I don't remember who, realized that we were the only church who had ever had both Life Action and the Suteras. When Del realized this, he wanted to have a meeting to compare the two. We scheduled a one-day meeting at the Holiday Inn Conference room in Niles, Michigan. Del, Byron Paulus, and I met. As we looked at both efforts, the heart was the same – many of the Scriptures were the same, but the approach was different. Life Action started low and built to a great climax, whereas the Suteras started, as I said, with a bang and then settled into teaching, which left the ministry in a revived but more normal sense.

The bottom line of our discussion was the constant need for definition of the terms and realities of the transforming power of the gospel. That meeting was really encouraging because of the humility and acceptance of both Del and Byron. It clarifies the obvious need for pastoral teaching which I sensed I was called to do. In a multitude of counselors, there is safety.

16
Oliver Price and The Bible Prayer Fellowship Connection
(February 1988)

*"Behold, I stand at the door and knock; if any man
hear my voice, and open the door, I will come in
to him, and will sup with him, and he with Me."*
                                        −Revelation 3:20

Joe, I'm speaking on Jesus Christ obviously
present and actively in charge.   −Oliver Price

After the Suteras left, we relaxed through Thanksgiving Day but
dialogued a lot about future priorities. We decided as a congregation
to make prayer our first line of defense and offense. We had prayer
meetings, but we really weren't a praying church. We sought counsel
from the Suteras and others.

Ralph and Lou were masters at involving others in their ministry.
They could effectively be called "Bridge People" who connect
people in ministry. In January 1988, just after our meeting, they
went to a Baptist Church in Fort Worth, Texas. While there they
met a gentleman named Oliver Price, who headed up a prayer
ministry in Dallas called Bible Prayer Fellowship. Knowing of our
desire to pray, Lou called and told me about Oliver and invited me
to join them and share my testimony which we did.

Oliver was just as Lou had described. He had a huge welcoming
smile and a heart for prayer. I would add he also had a brilliant mind

and was clothed with humility. We hit it off and immediately became kindred spirits. I invited him to come and speak to our church on prayer and

Joe, I'm going to speak on Jesus Christ obviously present and actively in charge.

give us some ideas about how to become a praying church. A few days before the meeting, I called to get his message titles for our church bulletin. He said, **"Joe, I'm going to speak on Jesus Christ obviously present and actively in charge."**

When he said that, my whole world focused! It was like all the lenses of my spiritual camera focused. Del Fehsenfeld had told me almost three years earlier, "If you ask 80 different people to define revival, you will get 80 different answers." He was right. So when Oliver said, "Jesus Christ obviously present and actively in charge," those eight words have become for me the answer to everything. For me it is the definition for revival. Any wretched circumstance or pathetic relationship is healed when the parties involved allow Jesus to be welcomed and in charge. **Revival happens when we practice the presence of Christ through Scripture-based praying.**

If you have read the whole story up until now, you realize Jesus had become my life, and now I was given a glimpse of how He wanted to be the Life of our church. From that day to this, I have been an avid student of how to operate under the active headship of Jesus as a pastor. Having received over 2 decades of mentoring from Oliver, the grace of God has impassioned me to carefully study Scripture while observing the life of the body of Christ and learn how to pastor with Christ obviously present and actively in charge. My search, as stated earlier, was to answer the question, "How can I allow Christ to build His church (Matt. 16:18) and still maintain responsible leadership?" Please understand I'm speaking here about a local church – specifically the one I am called to serve. The mind of Christ on a universal level is beyond my experience. So I'm speaking to the ordinary pastor who, like me, is in the trenches, engaged in hand-to-hand combat for the power of the gospel and the glory of God. There is, however, one more piece to the story – sovereign placement.

17
A Frowning Providence Made Plain
(My Wife Died)

*"So I spake unto the people in the morning;
and at evening my wife died, and I did in
the morning as I was commanded."*
–Ezekiel 24:18

"Blind unbelief is sure to err and scan His
work in vain; God is His own interpreter,
and He will make it plain." –William Cowper

As we practiced the active headship of Christ, the ministry continued to grow and change for God's glory. As I reflect on those years, it is clear that we were blessed with both God's face and His hand. I am enriched from having been a part of His kindness.

At the center of this development was simply a growing prayer closet. Through the two revival efforts, we netted a core of believers who really believed that what they believed about Jesus was really real. They became leaders of leaders according to II Timothy 2:2. Faithful men were teaching faithful men. Thus the infrastructure of the church was built around keeping Jesus as our first love. I sensed my role to be that of a spiritual cupid, intent on keeping our leadership hotly pursuing a passion for Christ, always relying on His sufficiency.

The ministry continued to be healthy but not extremely large. We kept a Christ-centered philosophy, developed a Spirit-filled leadership, birthed Spirit-led, Bible-based ministry programs which remained flexible, and built adequate facilities as needed to serve the ministry functions while remaining debt free. Two outstanding qualities of this body were patience and perseverance They were a delight to me. In many, many ways, together we saw Christ-centered dreams come true. We all worked very hard, but we did it by grace and not by grudge.

In 1995, my wife DiAnne contracted breast cancer and fought a noble battle for 7 years. This would be the way she would glorify God in her death on November 16, 2002, at 10:22 p.m. All of us were around her bed when she quietly slipped into the presence of the Lord. Her beloved twin sister DeLoris, who served as our nurse during her final year, was also there. She was a God-send for our family.

She was a mom's mom to many through the years. Her children all married godly mates and have borne 13 grandchildren, who are being nurtured in the ways of the Lord. It was a privilege to be her husband for nearly 36 years.

One time during our courting years, she was playing the piano, and we were singing together. We were singing a hymn, "The Solid Rock." We came to the line, "I dare not trust the sweetest frame but wholly lean on Jesus' name." She stopped playing and singing, nudged me firmly with her right arm and said, "That's you, buddy!" I didn't get it at first, but quickly realized that she was telling me that I would always play second fiddle to Jesus in her life. As we both embraced that truth, we found it to be the foundation for our lives, our marriage, our parenting, and our ministry. Thank you, DiAnne.

After her passing, I found myself a single grandpa at home, and I felt the church needed a younger man with a family. In July of 2003, I resigned the church and went on the road full-time giving prayer seminars in local churches. God had provided the freedom to do this and had proven these principles of pastoring and prayer really did work for the production of lasting fruit and the glory of God without the wood, hay, and stubble. I didn't want to go on the road with some message that didn't work at home. God blessed my schedule, and for 5 years, I traveled non-stop.

During this time, I began to develop a relationship with a lady who actually came to our church as a widow and trusted the Lord. We began to see each other in a group fellowship of widows and widowers who would go out together on Friday nights for dinner just to have company. The more I saw her, the more I liked what I saw. Knowing there is no fool like an old fool, I had to know that I had God's permission to pursue her as a mate. Before Teresa became a follower of Jesus, she was divorced. Her first husband left her after 5 years of marriage. She remained single for several years then married and was widowed after 5 years. The pastor who performed her second wedding was a close friend to her late husband's family. He brought her to our church after the death, and during the spring of that year, she repented and trusted Jesus. I baptized her a few weeks later. The divorce in her past gave me some pause so we waited, sought counsel, stayed pure, and actively sought the Lord until God gave the green light. In January of 2007, after Wednesday prayer meeting, I asked her to marry me as I washed her feet and promised to cleanse her as a servant-husband. We were married on April 14, 2007. Teresa is a delight to me. After 8 years, our union has proven to be life-giving. She is an avid student of God's Word and actively pursues ministry to God's people. "He who finds a wife finds a good thing and obtains favor of the Lord" (Prov. 18:22). Surely God has shown me favor in my old age.

This moved me to her home in West Lebanon, Indiana. I continued to travel, and when off the road, I sought fellowship with local pastors by taking them to lunch. On the road, I missed the camaraderie of a staff. One of my new pastor friends was the pastor of First Baptist Church in Covington, where the original Life Action meeting took place.

He confided in me that the church was struggling, and he was tired. I simply served him as I could by doing physical chores. One day he asked me if I would fill the pulpit while he took a break. I agreed to do so, and during that very week I was scheduled to speak, he resigned! I asked him if he still wanted me to speak, and he graciously responded, "Yes, they will need somebody." God put me, after 23 years, into the very church where he had shown Himself strong in revival with a fresh opportunity to pastor that church with Christ obviously present and actively in charge. *Reader, this is a providential miracle of God which I never imagined or sought for!* A few months later they officially installed me as their pastor. Teresa and I watched the life of the Vine take over the soul of this church.

From here, I will attempt to share the practical Biblical theology that releases the life of Christ in a local ministry. There has been great joy in this journey.

SECTION THREE

The Life of the Vine in the Prayer Life of the Church

A Practical Theology of Corporate Prayer

18
The Power of Praying Together

"Behold I stand at the door and knock.
If any man hear my voice, and open the
door, I will come into him and will sup
*with him, and he with Me." –*Revelation 3:20

"Truly successful families and ministries
eagerly meet with Jesus as a community." –jch

This chapter is being presented before and apart from the seven stewardships because it is the Driver of everything else. We can't even see the Kingdom movements without a developing intimacy with Jesus through Scripture-based praying as a church community.

Paul carefully instructed Timothy that before "all their doings" the church must pray (I Tim. 2:1). Jesus made this terrific offer to the church of Laodicea, that if they would hear His knocking and open the door, He would come to dinner and stay as long as they wanted in intimate dialogue. For those of us who crave fellowship with Jesus and long for the "glass darklies" to be removed, this is an offer beyond all imagination. So why don't we run our churches from the table with Jesus?

A few years ago while we were watching *"The Truth Project"* produced by Focus on the Family, Dr. Del Thackett asked the question, **"Do you really believe that what you believe is really real?"** In my opinion, I'm not sure how many Christians really believe that Jesus' offer is really real. I do. I love to dialogue with Spirit-filled friends over a welcoming table of food. From personal experience, nothing has blessed my life as consistently as a family meal. I have enjoyed the presence of some outstanding guests. How much more for the guest to be Jesus!

To the reader I would say this chapter is the most important chapter in the book because it will enable Christ to birth ministry through you as a pastor and people from His active administrative place in the Godhead. While we will never produce a second Pentecost, we can operate under the same administration which started then and should continue until this day. **Jesus Himself is the chief operating officer of His church which He purchased with His own blood.**

After the outpouring of the Spirit in Acts 2, listen to Peter's explanation: "Therefore being by the right hand of God exalted, and having received of the Father the promise of the Holy Ghost, _He hath shed forth this, which ye now see and hear,_" (Acts 2:33). An understanding of this will offer a whole new understanding of corporate prayer. We must never attempt to build the church without consistent dialogue with her Head, Jesus.

A.W. Tozer asks a haunting question to the church. "Is He your Lord or merely a beloved symbol?" Is He an active head or a figurehead? I would also ask, what is the difference between headship and lordship? The answer is Lordship can be detached but headship cannot. Someone can be a lord and not be an organic part of the group he overlords. Headship requires constant connection or else the beheaded body dies. The church's life comes from her head which dictates a life-flowing connection. That being said, we could begin to answer two questions:

1. Why should a church pray together?
2. Why should a believer be an intentional part of the prayer life of his/her church?

From my own experience and by their own admission, individuals, families, and churches hunger for the reality of God, that is, experiencing God doing things that can only be explained by Him.

God's laser beam of provision in meeting a specific need lets us know that He knows our address and is on location with us.

One time I did a survey of young men asking them what discouraged them most about praying. The most frequent answer was, "I don't see that it makes that much difference." I appreciated their honesty and set out to remove the discouraging distractions of the normal prayer meeting and give real reasons why praying together always made a difference. Let's start with the threefold main frame that makes sense of corporate prayer. We should pray together:

1. Because of who Jesus is.
2. Because of who the church is.
3. Because of what prayer is.

"Who is Jesus?"

1. **Jesus Christ obviously present and actively in charge is our paradigm for success.** Why? **Because the natural by-product of His activity is lasting fruit.** In one short verse, He both promises and warns us. "I am the Vine, ye are the branches: He that abideth in Me, and I in him, the same bringeth forth much fruit; for without Me ye can do nothing" (John 15:5). The fruitfulness of the church is determined by its intentional practice of abiding in the vine. The barrenness of the church is most often found in its prayer-less busyness.

   In the last 50 years, I have observed many trendy paradigms which have offered to build great churches or at least grow their attendance: bus ministries, big day events, church growth, visitation nights, seeker sensitive, emergent church, etc. Admittedly these all have some good ideas and good advice. But the **good news of real church increase is found in her Head, Jesus.** So we must return to the original paradigm: that Jesus left us, "And, behold, I send the promise of My Father upon you; but tarry ye in the city of Jerusalem, until ye be endued with power from on high" (Luke 24:49). Jesus was saying, "Stay in touch, stay connected." So the disciples honored and obeyed His instructions and continued

*T*he good news of real church increase is found in her Head, Jesus.

with one accord in prayer (Acts 1:14), and when the day of Pentecost was fully come, they were all with one accord in one place (Acts 2:1). After Jesus sent the Holy Spirit at Pentecost, "they (still) continued steadfastly in the apostles' doctrine and fellowship, and in the breaking of bread, and in prayers (Acts 2:42). This precedent set by Jesus through those early believers becomes the template for Scripture-based corporate praying which enables the church to abide in the Vine and bring forth much fruit. This is the original paradigm for success.

Let's notice the historical progression of the relationship of Jesus to the church as revealed in Scripture.

In Matthew 16:18, Jesus promises to build His church upon who He is. At that time, Jesus was on the earth and the disciples were on the earth. Jesus was present and authoritatively in charge. After His ascension we find the disciples on earth and Jesus in heaven. After a period of ten days, on the day of Pentecost, Jesus sent forth the Holy Spirit in great power. "This Jesus hath God raised up, whereof we all are witnesses. Therefore being by the right hand of God exalted, and having received of the Father the promise of the Holy Ghost, He hath shed forth this, which ye now see and hear." Again Jesus was present and in charge (Acts 2:32, 33). Jesus was birthing and building His church from heaven. In fact, in Mark 16:20, we read that after Jesus was received up into heaven and was sitting at the right hand of God... "they went forth, and preached every where, **the Lord working with them**, and confirming the Word with signs following." He was present and in charge from the Throne.

Fast forward to Revelation Chapter 1 and we see Jesus, the Son of Man, walking in the midst of the seven candlesticks which are the seven churches (Rev. 1:10-20). The glorified Christ is still walking in the midst of His church. He is still present and in charge. **The potential of having Christ present and in charge fascinates my faith!**

The potential of having Christ present and in charge fascinates my faith!

If we could grasp the possibilities of this cooperation with Christ in prayer that believes and practices His presence in the midst of our churches, it could revive and revolutionize our ministries. This thought has totally changed my life. I so want to pass it on. Let me encourage younger ministers to avoid getting caught up in the tools of the latest trend and miss the Carpenter Himself.

The first and primary work of the church is faith in Jesus Christ (John 6:26-29). Churches start going bad when they leave their first love for Jesus (Revelation 2:4). The Ephesian church was doing everything else right, but they had left their first love and were in danger of extinction brought on by the Lord Himself (Rev. 2:5).

It's Not My Church

After our first reviving with Life Action, the church entered a bit of a slump in attendance and offerings, but we were also experiencing the expressions of new found life. People spoke openly of their struggles and their victories. The walls had come down, the roof had come off and believers were learning to be transparent with God and the church body. This made the "establishment" uncomfortable. They called a meeting and wanted me there.

It was a cold, gray Illinois day in early spring. After some cordial greetings, the interrogation began.

"Can you tell us why the attendance is down?" I said, "No."

"Can you tell us why the offerings are down?" I said, "No."

"We know why you took the attendance board down. You didn't want us to see everything dropping. Furthermore you have turned our church into a Catholic Holy-Roller church." This was deduced from the open testimonies coupled with the new praise chorus we learned. People were now praising joyfully. I had taken the attendance board down because nearly every week I heard members of the choir making so many comments about the attendance. If we were up a little, they were elated. If we were down, they were deflated. I just really thought the focus should be on Jesus, at least for the Sunday morning worship.

Everyone sat in awkward silence. Feeling like I should say something to account for the sagging attendance and offering, I began to query.

"Have I been immoral?" They said, "No, not that we know of."

"Have I mishandled any money?" They said, "No."

"Have I preached the Word?" "Yes."

"Have I loved the people?" "Yes."

After a long pause and silence, God gave me these words. "I don't know what the actual problem is. I don't have the answers. All I can say is, it's not my church. It belongs to Jesus."

When I said that, it seemed like a gentle breeze blew into the room. We all seemed relieved that somehow we were beginning to recognize Jesus as the owner and the builder of His church. It was a definite turning point in our ministry. For the next 18 years, we became "underservants" together, cooperating with Jesus as He worked. At the core, we moved from being owners to being stewards. The strangle-hold of human pride is broken when Jesus alone is embraced as the Head of the church. It was a life-changing moment for our leadership. From there we never looked back.

Selah – Pause for a moment and reflect on the possibilities of Jesus being obviously present and actively in charge of your stewardship.

2. **Jesus Christ obviously present and actively in charge is our platform for conflict resolution. Why? Because the spontaneous response to His presence is a devastating humility.**

My biggest fear in ministry over the years has been that the sheep will begin to fight each other, and I will not be able to stop the fighting. There is nothing worse than to be preaching your heart out, all the while knowing that there is an undercurrent of division in the congregation that snuffs out the fire of every word you say. Satan is a divider. He hands everyone their ammunition yet declares himself neutral. He uses distraction, discouragement, and deflection. **Churches and homes split because they don't agree upon a platform to be used to resolve conflicts.** Scripturally, Jesus is that platform.

In Matthew 18:15-20, Jesus gives us clear instructions in how to settle our offenses. Verse 20, which is often used out of context says, "For where two or three are gathered together in My name, there am I in the midst of them." Jesus promises to be the humbling presence to those who meet to be right with God and each other. In John 17:20-23, He prays for the love, the oneness, and the glory of the Godhead to be ours in relationships.

Someone's Presence Makes a Difference

Whether it's a hand in the cookie jar or driving too fast on the freeway, someone's presence makes a difference. The sight of a State Trooper parked just over the hill can cause a speeding motorist to slow down immediately. One time some families were complaining to me about what was going on in their church. After a moment I asked them, "If the glorified Christ walked into our midst, what would we do?" Immediately they said, "We would fall on our faces before Him." Great men like Isaiah, Ezekiel and Daniel crumbled in the presence of the glory of God. In the presence of God, attitudes change from "What's wrong with them?" to "Woe is me."

In Revelation 1:12, the beloved Apostle John turned to see who was speaking to him, and when he saw Him (v. 17), He said, "I fell at His feet as dead." This dear disciple that leaned on Jesus' breast at the Last Supper could not stand in the presence of His majesty. The practiced presence of Jesus cleanses and humbles every proud worshiper. I might add it also comforts. Jesus then touched John with His right hand and reminded him of whom He was (v. 17, 18). What a scene.

Here is a model for our attitude in prayer as we meet to settle our offenses. With all parties in agreement:

1. Let us welcome His presence. (This is a practiced presence.)
2. Let us ask Him to take charge.
3. Let us ask Him to change each individual. (There is often a rub here because most of the time we blame others. But we must be 100 percent responsible for whatever percent we are wrong, even if it is a small percentage.)
4. Let us ask Him to bring us into harmony with the Father and with each other.

I have used this format many times and watched God melt the pride of strong men and women and renew the oneness they had forgotten they had in Christ.

My hobby is playing the piano. I play mostly hymns and simple songs I learned as a young Christian. But I especially enjoy playing when the piano is in tune. It's discouraging to me to try to produce pretty music from an untuned piano. If a tuner comes, in order to bring the instrument up to pitch, he must tune all 88 keys to one standard tuning fork. When he does, a musician is able to then bring forth beautiful harmonies with rich chords.

So it is with the church. When each member is changed in the presence of Jesus and brought into harmony with the Father, a rich song breaks forth for the glory of God and for a witness to the world.

Selah: Pause right now and meditate on the potential harmony of our homes and our churches if we practiced the presence of Christ in our conflict resolution.

"When I survey the wondrous cross
On which the Prince of glory died,
My richest gain I count but lost,
And pour contempt on all my pride."

3. **Jesus Christ obviously present and actively in charge is our promise for life's ultimate fulfillment because our life is replaced by His life.**

Every one of us could chuckle at the ways we have looked for fulfillment. My list of notable fulfillers starting with childhood would include: Playing with my dog Ring, sandbox farm implements under the big maple by the well, driving a team of horses, riding my pony pretending to be Roy Rogers (The King of Cowboys), Zoro, or running out to warm up before a grade school basketball game. Later it was getting my driver's license, having a car and a girlfriend. On the farm, it was driving heavy equipment watching the diesel smoke roll and smelling freshly plowed soil or fresh cut hay. As life goes along, it becomes having a wife and children and enough money to pay the bills and finally retirement. Even in gospel ministry, we can seek satisfaction from big audiences or busy programs with the hope that something's happening. All of these can become subtle substitutes for the one thing that really satisfies and that is being transformed in the presence of Jesus. I love Psalm 16:11, "Thou wilt show me the path of life: in Thy presence is fullness of joy; at Thy right hand there are pleasures forevermore."

Reading Jesus' Letters

In Revelations chapters 2 and 3, we have seven letters which Jesus relates to the seven churches of Asia Minor, now Turkey. Here we only want to look at their format. Each one includes four main points that Jesus wanted to emphasize. In each one, Jesus said:

1. "Let Me introduce Myself – here's who I am." These statements were tailor-made for each church and exalted the magnitude of Christ's character.
2. "Let Me tell you what I know." Every time I read these letters and notice how Jesus says, "I know Thy works," I am thrilled to my core because I believe that Jesus and He alone really does know the true condition of any church that I am called to shepherd. No church consultant can match His omniscience. This gives me great hope in prayer.
3. "Let me correct and instruct you; please listen carefully." The words, "Repent – or else," followed by "He that hath an ear let him hear," should give us an immediate pause and call us to give undivided attention to the Master builder. **Listening is the biggest part of the praying dialogue.**
4. "Let me comfort and encourage you with hope." **Jesus wants us to succeed but we must cooperate with His design.** Jesus does not bless independent, individualistic sub-contractors. He wants a relationship in the process. To Him the process is as important as the end product. The design and date of completion are His, but He is strategically interested in our joy and encouragement as laborers. He calls us overcomers. He knows our need for His approval and reward.

"Guess Who's Coming to Supper"

In Jesus' final letter written to the church of the Laodiceans, He includes all four elements of the first six letters plus one more that especially gives us hope and a way forward. To this very rich and proud church who had grown nauseatingly lukewarm to Jesus, He made an amazing almost too good to be true offer. Here it is. "Behold I stand at

Life's ultimate privilege is Jesus at my table.

the door, and knock: if any man hear my voice and open the door, I will come into him, and will sup with him, and he with Me." (Revelation 3:20). The "Head" of the church, the "Life" of the church, the "Purchaser" of the church, the "Builder" of the church is offering Himself to be at our table as we attempt to be the church. After rebuking them in love (v. 19), He gives a hearty "Behold" to let them know His eagerness for them to grasp this offer. He's excited about the possibilities. So He takes His position at the door of this church and politely knocks, wondering if there is a remnant who even has the spiritual ability to hear. In short, Jesus, the ultimate church consultant, is initiating a one-on-one, unhurried, fellowship supper with you, your family and your church! Think of the potential of these welcomed encounters.

Down through the years, we have had many very resourceful servants of God at our dinner table. They helped us raise our children. Hearing the life stories of these faithful servants helped anchor our souls in the Kingdom. One time, I arranged an afternoon with Dr. Warren Wiersbe. For 4 hours, we talked. I loved it. We had evangelists, revivalists, veteran missionaries, and Bible teachers fellowship with us and then graciously pray over us. Just for them to grace us with their presence has made such a difference. How much more, if the guest is Jesus. I love to say that **life's ultimate privilege is Jesus at my table.** Guess what? He wants to be there. So through Jesus we can have at our meetings:

1. God's Holy character – where revival begins
2. God's omnisciently accurate evaluation of our family or church condition
3. God's all wise solutions
4. God's promised blessing and reward

I might add – all free just for opening the door.

At this point, we have moved from Jesus Christ obviously present and actively in charge to <u>praying</u> with Jesus Christ obviously present and actively in charge. This is to be command central for our homes and churches. Make sure you go all the way to Jesus.

Let's make a final observation from this letter to the Laodicea church (Rev. 3:14-21). As I studied this letter in the context of the actual landscape of today's church, I can identify four distinct groups which represent four attitudes of prayer.

<u>Group #1</u> – These are "rich, and increased with goods, and have need of nothing (v. 17a). They think they have no need so <u>they pray without heart</u>. They are self-centered and self-sufficient.

<u>Group #2</u> – This group embraces their identity from Jesus as "wretched, and miserable, and poor, and blind, and naked" (v. 17b), and they get stuck there, seemingly unable to move on. They are overwhelmed with need so <u>they pray without hope</u>. They are problem-centered. The pride of self-pity is seldom recognized. Its chains are strong and deceitful.

<u>Group #3</u> – These zealots get their fire from Jesus' words in verse 19. "As many as I love, I rebuke and chasten; be zealous therefore, and repent." So they launch with all good intention to take back the kingdom of their own hearts by force. <u>They pray without rest</u> because they are works-centered. All of these so far, I call subtle substitutes for Jesus.

<u>Group #4</u> – The fourth group hears the knock, opens the door, and feasts on Jesus' presence. They are true worshipers. <u>They pray with heart, and hope, and rest</u> because they are Christ-centered. This is the place where individuals, families, and churches thrive with love, joy, peace, and lasting fruit.

We need to make sure our praying takes us all the way to Jesus.

There is a quaint connection between verses 20 and 21. Jesus follows His offer in verse 20 with a promise in verse 21. "To him that overcometh will I grant to sit with Me in my Throne, even as I also overcame, and am set down with My Father in His Throne." The lifestyle of heaven will be that of an intimate setting with the

Godhead. Don't ask me how that works. Modeling that setting on earth makes perfect sense and will prove to be a perfect way to execute kingdom living and ministry.

Transformed

For those readers who may think I am a hopeless mystic, this part may encourage you. Those who know me know that I love expository preaching that presents a clear message from the interpretation of a Scripture in its context. I am not a mystic, but I am trying to understand the mystery of Christ in us, the hope of glory. So take heart and let me rush to the believer's ultimate privilege in the presence of Jesus.

We pray best with our Bibles open.

First of all, let me say, prayer will always be boring and powerless if it's only a monologue, i.e., us talking to God. Oh, the dread of my early experience in prayer meetings. After a Bible study, prayer requests (mostly outer man needs) would go on and on. We would break into groups: men with men and women with women. The men would pray around the circle basically repeating all the same requests with varying clichés. They talked and repeated and informed God of all these things He evidently wasn't aware of – all with our heads bowed and eyes closed! I still don't like it to be that way. Prayer is meant to be a dialogue where listening to God becomes as much a part as talking to God. Praying for the strength of the inner man is always better than just praying for the healing of the outer man. "The spirit of a man will sustain his infirmity; but a wounded spirit who can bear" (Proverbs 18:14).

Secondly, the best way to listen to God is through His written Word. We pray best with our Bibles open – and maybe with our eyes open! Why not? Let's say our church is praying about the marriages of our families. Why not open our Bibles to classic passages on marriage and formulate prayers from the verses in front of us? Why not take time in prayer meetings to write prayers on 3x5 cards, then read our freshly crafted thoughts back to God in the hearing of our fellow prayer warriors? It sure beats vain repetition and shallow thoughts off the top of our heads.

I heard one Bible teacher say, "If I pray from my mind, I generally pray for only a few minutes. If I pray from my heart, I can pray longer. If I pray from Scripture, I can pray all day." How true. I used to think Bible study and prayer had to be two separate things. For many years now I have lumped them together, meditating on the text and praying for it to be true of my life and the life of our church. I truly pray best with my Bible open.

<u>Finally, if done right, we will be transformed in the place of prayer.</u> To be like Him is the goal and privilege of our praying. The entrance of God's Word gives light and understanding (Psalm 119:130). Here's a verse I cherish that gives me great hope for my life and our churches. *"But we all, with open face beholding as in a glass the glory of the Lord, <u>are changed</u> into the same image from glory to glory, even as by the Spirit of the Lord"* (II Cor. 3:18). Warren Wiersbe says it best. **"When the child of God, looks into the Word of God and sees the Son of God, he is changed into the image of God, by the Spirit of God for the glory of God."**

Here's the point. Humbly praying Scripture back to the Lord transforms the individual and the church who practices the same. Our wandering hearts are most satisfied when we realize that our metamorphosis results in our life being replaced by His. Beholding our transformation is life's ultimate fulfillment. This is what happens when we pray and humbly engage the Scriptures with Christ obviously present and actively in charge. If believers and churches want to change, this is where it starts. Transformation and ongoing revival can be the experience of any church who humbly prays with Bibles open.

Those sad and confused disciples on the road to Emmaus (Luke 24) were empowered with burning hearts (v. 32) because Jesus began at Moses and all the prophets and explained all the Scriptures concerning Himself. He opened the Scriptures to them. Soon they would join with the others and be used to turn the world upside down (Acts 17:6). This Jesus is the first and foremost reason for being an intentional part of the prayer life of your church.

Who is the Church?

After 50 years of ministry, I am hopelessly fascinated with the potential of the church. This, of course, begins with the previous discussion of who Jesus is in the midst of His church. But my excitement grows as I consider what God has ordained the church to be, we can become.

The church is God's new community in whom He has chosen to dwell and through whom He has chosen to work.

The church was:
- Conceived in the heart of the Father before the foundation of the world (Eph. 1:4)
- Bought by the blood of the Son slain from the foundation of the world (Acts 20:28, Rev. 13:8)
- Birthed by the moving of the Spirit – 3,000 at one time! (Acts 2)
- Delivered by the preaching of the apostles (Acts 2; Eph. 2:19-22)
- She now grows under the authority of her active Head, Jesus (Matt. 16:8, Col. 2:19)
- She will be caught up to meet her Groom (I Thess. 4:13-18)
- She will be robed in white (Rev. 19:8)
- She will marry the Lamb (Rev. 19:6-9)
- She will live happily ever after with her first love! (I Thess. 4:17, 18; Rev. 22:1-5)

I don't know about you, but I think that's a pretty fair list of supernatural endowments! And we the redeemed are in on it. Plus it's an organism – a living, breathing, growing, functioning organism powered by the resurrected life of Christ. All three members of the Godhead are directly vested in her. Why shouldn't we be excited about who we are? Remove this beauty from the earth, and all that is left is a perverse generation from which we have been saved. The world may lump us all together and treat us like common grocery stores, gas stations, and fast food restaurants or even a nuisance that is weak and poor, but we have a secret treasure in these "clay pots" – His name is Jesus. **Even believing church members of our local churches would do well to raise the value of their own belief system about their faith community. We are the gospel culture of every tribe and nation.**

In summary, the <u>church is God's new community in whom He has chosen to dwell and through whom He has chosen to work</u>.

Throughout Bible history, God has been in the business of starting new communities. He started with Adam and Eve. He started again after the Flood with Noah and his family. Then He called Abraham after the confusion of the languages to begin again with his family which grew to be the nation of Israel. Now after Israel rejected Jesus, God set them aside and birthed the church – His new community.

Her dramatic birth on the day of Pentecost brought 3,000 souls into the church at once, and He continues to add to the church daily such as should be saved (Acts 2:37-47).

The church is also God's <u>habitation</u> on earth through the Spirit. I used to listen to the old time preachers talk about the Shekinah Glory of God coming down on the tabernacle as God dwelt among His people and think, "Where does God dwell today?" Listen to this, "Now therefore ye are no more strangers and foreigners, but fellow citizens with the saints, and of the household of God; And are built upon the foundation of the apostles and prophets, Jesus Christ Himself being the chief cornerstone; In whom all the building fitly framed together groweth unto an holy temple in the Lord. In whom ye also are builded together for an **habitation of God** through the Spirit (Eph. 2:19-22).

People should be able to drive into our town looking for God and come to the assembly of our church and find Him! In his instruction to Timothy, Paul clearly says, *"These things write I unto thee, hoping to come unto thee shortly: But if I tarry long, that thou mayest know how thou oughtest to behave thyself in the house of God, which is the church of the living God, the pillar and ground of the truth"* (I Tim.y 3:14, 15). Do you see why we should love and cherish the church? In this one living organism we have God, God's truth, and God's community of people.

After Pentecost, these believers pursued the heart of Jesus as a group. They went public, upward, and forward together.

> Then they that gladly received His word were baptized:
> And the same day there were added unto them about
> Three thousand souls. And they continued steadfastly
> In the apostles doctrine and fellowship, and in breaking
> Of bread, and in prayers. –Acts 2:41, 42

1. They believed the same truth. (Doctrine)
2. They shared the same love. (Fellowship)
3. They embraced the same covenant. (Breaking of bread)
4. They trusted the same source. (Prayer)
5. They were committed to the same cause. (To know Christ and make Him known)

Together they enjoyed purpose, power, purity, and generosity. God was adding to the church daily according to His sovereign grace (Acts 2:47). They feared the Lord, they were together, and no one lacked because the great grace of God was on them all (Acts 4:33).

But Something Happened!

Enter stage right Ananias and Sapphira, his wife, with their own personal agenda (Acts 5:1-11). Wanting to get in on the action, they were overcome by their own pretense. Satan wanted someone, like in the Garden of Eden, who was a part of this dynamic church organism to perform one independent act which would in turn give him permission, a place to set up a stronghold of pride and stop the power of grace. Death came to both parties, and great fear came upon all the church. **Individualism, with its disrespect and disregard for the active headship of Jesus over His faith community (the church), had the spirit of a suicide bomber.**

What is the fastest growing sin in the evangelical church (North America) that cooperates with society in helping to pave the way for the antichrist?

Individualism – unwillingness to submit and be accountable with the body to Jesus is rendering our local churches powerless and full of disaster.

Prayer, the divine "spinal cord" between Christ and His church.

The sin of **individualism** is most dangerous because it appears so respectable yet allows the individualist to create God in his or her own image. **Through individualism we destroy the God-ordained theocracy of the church.** Our churches begin to look like the culture, and our faith stands in the wisdom of men, rather than the power of Christ. We lose the privilege and encouragement that comes from God's demonstration of the Spirit and power. (I Cor. 2:1-5).

Thus we should repent of our private Christianity and join in the shared – relationship with Jesus and our church to pray. Any church who will intentionally practice this will experience blessings limited only by the sovereignty of God.

Oh Lord allow our posture together under
The headship of Jesus pave the way for you
to show up and shake the place with Your approval. –Acts 4:31

What is Prayer?

"If prayer stands as the place where God and human beings meet, then I must learn about prayer. Most of my struggles in the Christian life circle around the same two themes: Why God doesn't act the way we want God to, and why I don't act the way God wants me to. Prayer is the precise point where those themes converge."
–Philip Yancey

In this short treatment of prayer, we are only going to look at its practical function in the relationship between Christ, the Head of the church and the church itself which is His body. **In this context, I call prayer the divine spinal cord between Christ and His church.** Jesus never intended for His "left behind" remnant to lose connection with Him even though He ascended back to the Father. His instructions were, "And, behold, I send the promise of My Father upon you: but tarry ye in the city of Jerusalem, until ye be endued with power from on high" (Luke 24:49). So they all continued with one accord in prayer and supplication both men and women. When the day of Pentecost came, they were all with one accord in one place. They never allowed their connection with Jesus to go unattended or merely assumed it was healthy. Their physical face-to-face connection had come to an end but their first class prayer connection was just beginning. The new prayer connection would have to be much superior because Jesus could now communicate with His church through the Holy Spirit in multiple locations around the world. This connection with Jesus was the disciple's lifeline in the newly initiated church and still is. **Without good Bible-based communication with Jesus, we leave our active connection with the Head and can expect paralysis, spiritual spasms or even the death of a ministry.**

We can all relate to high-profile people like Christopher Reeves (Superman) or Joni Erickson Tada, whose spinal cord injuries rendered them paralyzed. We know of people in our own lives with similar challenges. Likewise, Christian ministry suffers greatly if prayer, that connection between Christ and His church, is broken or weakened. Here are some key "Head and Body" verses that relate this vital message.

"And hath put all things under His feet, and gave Him to be head over all things to the church which is His body, the fulness of Him that filleth all in all." –Ephesians 1:22-23

"But speaking the truth in love, may grow up into Him in all things, which is the head, even Christ. From whom the whole body fitly joined together and compacted by that which every joint supplieth, according to the effectual working in the measure of every part, maketh increase of the body unto the edifying of itself in love." –Ephesians 4:15-16

"For the husband is the head of the wife, even as Christ is the head of the church;" –Ephesians 5:23a

"And not holding the Head, from which all the body by joints and bands having nourishment ministered, and knit together, increaseth with the increase of God." –Colossians 2:19

Let's put it all together. These passages leave no questions. The church receives resurrection power from her living Head. The Father gave Jesus to be the Head over all things to the church which is His body. His supply as the Head nourishes the fitly-joined members of the body, which in turn edifies itself in love and increases with the increase of God! I love to ask pastors, "How big do you think your church should be?" We pastors always like bigger. At least, I do. This Bible-based, Christ-centered corporate praying honors the living organic nature of the church, keeps the healthy connection between the body and her Head, and is the driving force behind all church ministry. It keeps the life of the Vine in the prayer life of the church. Bigger is not always better, and small is not sacred. The perfect size for any church is the size God wants it to be. If we "continue steadfastly" with Jesus Christ obviously present and actively in charge, our churches will increase with the increase of God and that is always right. This is not an endorsement of passivity but rather a pursuit of first love for Jesus in prayer.

One more thing. If we use the bride and groom analogy in Ephesians 5:23, we will enjoy seeing our Groom Jesus, functioning as the initiator of the grace activity, and the Church functioning as the faithful bride who responds excitedly to her lover.

Every believer needs to be intentionally involved in the prayer life of his or her church because of who Jesus is (the Head), who the church is (the Body), and what prayer is (the vital connection).

SECTION FOUR

The Life of the Vine
in the Soul of the Church

Introduction to Section 4: "The seven stewardships of Revival"

We have finally arrived at the explanation of the heart of this message for pastors and servants in the local church. I sincerely felt that this section could be best understood if you knew a little of its context. My prayer is that the next seven brief chapters will become a part of your story as servants of Christ and stewards of the mysteries of God (I Cor. 4:1). A knowledge of these stewardships would have clarified my understanding early on and would have helped me prepare the sheep for their journey with God as well. As a reminder, an understanding of these stewardships came during my search to answer the question, **"How can I allow Christ to build His church as He promised and still maintain responsible leadership?"**

The following chapters are timeless, not trendy. They fit any size congregation. They work in large cities, small towns, or country churches. They fit any culture. I have taught these principles in North America, South America, and Asia. No matter where they have been shared, they were received with the same encouraging response. They are meant to be "good news" which comes from the life of Christ and the power of His gospel opposed to "good advice" which may have applications only for a particular genre of church setting. They are not meant to be a "cookie cutter" methodology, and they are <u>not</u> new. In fact one time a local man commented on my teaching and said, "We really like Joe's teaching, but he just never says anything we don't already know!" And he was very sincere!

Knowing this, let me encourage you not to look at the newness of the truth but rather the order in which each truth appears. This will give us an idea of what our response should be to Jesus as He builds. We will know how to cooperate with Him as the Vine. In some ways, this is simply a stewardship of abiding on a corporate level.

"How can I allow Christ to build His church as He promised and still maintain responsible leadership?"

Remember, this is not about how a pastor builds a church; this is about how a pastor leads his congregation to cooperate with Jesus while allowing Him to build the church which He purchased with His own blood. The application of these is for a local congregation.

If Jesus Christ obviously present and actively in charge is our definition of revival, then a proper stewardship of His life and activity in our midst will allow revival to be the lifestyle of our church and will release the transforming power of the gospel. The potential of these seven stewardships is limited only by the sovereignty of God Himself.

Watch the order:

1. By grace
2. Through faith
3. In worship
4. In warfare
5. Through discipleship
6. Within the church
7. Into the world

19
By Grace

"...Paul and Barnabas: who, speaking to them,
persuaded them to continue in the grace of God."
—Acts 13:43

The life and authority of Christ invades the church
through divinely orchestrated acts of grace.
(The Stewardship of Grace)

<u>Our stewardship:</u> To observe carefully and
cherish what God initiates!

The revival of 1985 came to our region by the grace of God.
Notice Dr. Gregg Curtis' words as he reports on the revival. He was
the pastor of First Baptist in Covington at the time. "God visited
our church in a way that was totally unexpected and unplanned by
us.—We had prayed for revival but none of us really knew what we
were asking God to do. We received more than we expected – we got
what we needed!" (*Spirit of Revival*, August 1985).

God, by grace, is the initiator of all Kingdom activity. Our
effectiveness in ministry comes as we learn to observe His activity,
cherish what He is doing, and cooperate. Here's what Jesus the Vine
says to us, "Ye have not chosen Me, but I have chosen you, and and
ordained you, that ye should go and bring forth fruit, and that your
fruit should remain: that whatsoever ye shall ask of the Father in My
name, He may give it you" (John 15:16).

My ministry mindset immediately began to change the first time I heard Manley Beasley say, "Jesus never initiated anything but rather waited on His Father." Jesus Himself said, "My Father worketh hitherto, and I work" (John 5:17). Again, He reinforced, "Verily, verily, I say unto you, the Son can do nothing of Himself, but what He seeth the Father do: for what things so ever He doeth, these also doeth the Son likewise" (John 5:19). "I can of mine own self do nothing: as I hear, I judge: and my judgment is just; because I seek not Mine own will, but the will of the Father which hath sent Me" (John 5:30).

God, by grace is the initiator of all Kingdom activity.

Jesus is telling us that He obeyed the Father's will, did the Father's work and spoke the Father's words. God alone initiates anything that is eternal. We love Him because He first loved us (I John 4:19). History is always His-story. He chose to create, His grace found Noah, called Abraham and Moses and raised up the judges and the prophets. He ordained John the Baptist, sent Jesus through the Virgin, called Peter for the Jews and Paul for the Gentiles. He gave the Revelation of Jesus to Jesus and signified it by His angel unto His servant John (Rev. 1:1). So why, for years, did I think that I had to come up with genius ideas to sell them to my congregation, then whip them into action and make something happen for God? Because that was all I knew from the impressions I was given. Well-meaning, we were missing God's movement of grace.

To the church, Jesus has been given to be the active Head of all things (Eph. 1:22). He is the Groom who initiates and we the church are the bride who responds to Him as our beloved. So the life of the Vine enters the soul of the church by grace and we are blessed.

Grace brings salvation (Titus 2:11), teaches us to live godly (Titus 2:12,13), to give generously (2 Cor. 8:6), enables us to suffer joyfully (2 Cor. 12:9), and serve acceptably (Heb. 12:28). This is none other than the dynamic life of Christ in the soul of the church giving her the desire and power to obey God. I love Acts 4:33, which capsulizes the church condition. "And with great power gave the apostles witness of the resurrection of the Lord Jesus: and <u>great grace</u> was upon them all."

So where do church servants look for grace?

1. In every person who walks through the door. Where are they in their faith journey and how can the church serve them in taking the next step of faith? No respecter of persons, please, and don't forget the babies.

2. In open door opportunities. Be wise to distractions but alert to relationships.

3. Through heart changes. Testimonies from changed hearts can cross-pollinate spiritual growth in others and build a platform for ministry.

4. Through heart stirrings. God is in the business of calling out men like Paul and Barnabas to His work.

5. Through repentance and faith in salvation. Celebrations over the newly born again bring joy and encouragement. Make a big deal of the attitude of repentance.

6. Through natural and supernatural giftedness. Do a survey of gifts, passions, and callings. Give each person a place to use them. Empower and resource them for their ministry.

7. Through knowledge. Do your best to tap the intelligence of your congregation and show respect for their knowledge. Don't be afraid of the smart ones and don't belittle those who seem limited. Still water often runs deep and everyone knows something you don't.

8. Physical resources. Every church has resources available to them. We are more wealthy than we realize. The key is recognizing them as gifts from God to be employed in spreading the gospel. Don't "poor mouth" your congregation. Give them respect and dignity for who they are and what they have. Say "grace" over them.

9. Don't forget hardships. It is clear that God uses trials to build bridges which lead to relationships and ministry.

People admire your strengths, but they really relate to your weakness.

10. Other ministries – Don't be an island to yourself. No ministry is a know all, do all, self-sufficient fortress. We need to network, share resources, and partner with others who can bring to the table things we need but don't have. This helps the function of ministry and the attitude we reflect.

The list above is meant to get you started in looking for grace. There are many more. Just keep looking.

Let me finish this chapter with three short yet important reminders:

1. We can be steadfast and diligent while we are watching. After the great movement of God's grace initiative at Pentecost where 3,000 souls were saved, the church activity was described like this, **"And they continued steadfastly in the apostles' doctrine and fellowship, and in breaking of bread, and in prayers"** (Acts 2:42).

Since the Day of Pentecost, the four functioning operatives of the church have remained the same:

1. Scripture examination
2. Accountable fellowship
3. Gospel review and remembrance
4. Prayer connection with Jesus

Evangelism was a natural by-product which grew out of this transforming fellowship.

The point here is that, while we function by grace, we don't have to be "graced out" doing nothing while waiting on grace. God has clearly outlined our function and we can continue steadfastly in season and out of season.

I attended a revival conference once where the speaker was clearly emphasizing sovereign visitation of grace as in Jonathan

Edwards revivals. During an interactive time, one person asked, "What do we do in the meantime while we wait for such visitations?" The answer given has encouraged me through many dry seasons. "Be busy about the biblical disciplines of the church and preach the Word." That is sound advice that always stands the test of time and weathers any storm.

2. Cherish and treasure every morsel of grace made available by God no matter how small it seems. The Lord loves it when we really value His gifts. God loves a cheerful giver, but He also loves a thankful receiver. When talking about the Word of God, here's what Jesus said. "For whosoever hath, to him shall be given, and he shall have more abundance: but whosoever hath not, from him shall be taken away even that he hath" (Matt. 13:12). He gives this same truth in the parable of the talents (Matt. 25:29).

What does this mean to us who are seeking to be good stewards of God's grace initiatives in our lives? In the words of Matthew Henry, "There are those to whom this knowledge is not given, and a man can receive nothing unless it is given him from above (John 3:27) and be it remembered that God is debtor to no man; his grace is his own; he gives or withholds it at pleasure" (Rom. 11:35). The difference must be resolved into God's sovereignty. Note the rule God observes in dispensing His gifts. He bestows them on those who improve them but takes them away from those who bury them. Here is a promise to him that has true grace and uses what he has is promised more abundance."

Speak often of the grace God has given to your congregation. Help them see it, too. Celebrate God's gifts and invest them in Kingdom ministry. The motivational gifts in Romans 12:3-8 have been very helpful to me as I have sought to match gifts with ministry.

A few years ago, this idea of stewarding the grace you have was illustrated on a mission trip my wife and I took to Nicaragua. Our daughter Johanna and her husband Bob were ministering there, equipping Latino pastors for their work. One day, Bob and I visited one of the pastors who shepherded the flock who literally lived in the city dump. This was a congregation that lived resourcefully from what the city of Managua threw away, yet the pastor of the "Lathureka" trash heap found grace to have purpose and vision for his sheep. Grace always wins the day.

3. Never forget that humility always precedes grace in the lives of believers. A proud church will find itself fighting against the Lord Himself. "God resists the proud, but gives grace to the humble." (James 4:6). A church that continues well in the stewardship of grace must be vigilant about taking spiritual inventory starting with the leadership. No matter how well we may appear to be doing, we can still be failing because we have left the sense of our desperation for Jesus in a first-love relationship like the Ephesian church in Revelation We can be deceived into thinking that we are rich and increased with goods and have need of nothing like the Laodocean church in Revelation. Such an attitude can overtake us in our lack of awareness and make Jesus want to vomit, as you well know (Reve. 3:16). In the words of Del Fehsenfeld III, "Humility is the starting point for Life with God" (*Revive Magazine*, August 2015).

As a steward of God's grace, we will crouch low in humility, observe the gifts God gives, be thankful and cherish them for the treasures God meant them to be. Christ has invaded our church and given us direction through His gifts. We are now ready to respond and follow His moving through faith.

Never forget that humility always precedes grace.

20
Through Faith

"For unto us was the gospel preached, as well
As unto them, but the word preached did not
Profit them, not being mixed with faith in them
That heard it." –Hebrews 4:2

The life and authority of Christ is embraced by
definite acts of faith. (The Stewardship of Faith)

<u>Our stewardship:</u> To mix faith with everything –
the good, the bad, and the ugly.

We must never stop applying Scripture truth to any situation,
and we must never drop the shield of faith. "The first and primary
work of the church is faith in Jesus Christ." The first time I heard
Ian Murray say that, it stopped me in my tracks because that's not
what I had been taught. My thinking was more along the lines of
evangelism, discipleship or Bible instruction. So I shelved the idea
for a while until I realized that **faith in Christ's movements of
grace was the birth place of ministry functions.**

The heroes of the faith moved in faith to God's promptings of
grace and moved the gospel story along during their watch. Abel
offered a more excellent sacrifice by faith; Enoch was translated by
faith because of his grace to please God. Noah prepared an ark by
faith because of God's grace in a warning of things not yet seen. His
faith even had some fear in it. Abraham left home by faith because
of the grace of God's call. He wasn't sure where he was going, but he

was able to see, with the eyes of faith, a better city with a greater builder than anything he knew in Ur of Chaldees. (Heb. 11:1-10). You know the list goes on.

faith in Christ's movements of grace was the birth place of ministry functions.

Remember, the idea here is for us to steward the movements of God's grace by embracing them by faith and being Scripturally obedient in every one of them. The story God is writing in and through your church may appear like a mountain path that makes many hair pin turns while approaching the summit which, by the way, you may never see before the end of your watch. Once again, I cite our heroes, "These all died in faith, <u>not</u> having received the promises, but having seen them afar off, and were persuaded of them and embraced them, and confessed that they were strangers and pilgrims on the earth (Heb. 11:13). Yours may only be to see afar off but believing and obeying is yours for today. In fact, God makes it clear when He says, "But without faith it is impossible to please Him; for he that cometh to God must believe that He is, and that He is a rewarder of those who diligently seek Him" (Heb. 11:6). **A ministry that turns every movement and challenge into a treasure hunt for God will experience God's reward.** God has great plans in mind for a people who will call and pray and seek and search for Him with all their hearts (Jer. 29:11-13).

Sometimes our ministries do not appear to be doing that well. In fact, they may seem to be stalled or going backward – even after we have identified clear promises and directions of God's moving by grace. During these times it's really easy to second guess ourselves or slump in bewilderment over what God is doing or not doing. The prophet Habakkuk helps us out during these "death valley" days. His book starts with a bitter lament over Israel's condition. Godly King Josiah's reforms have been quickly overturned by his successor, Jehoiakim, and Habakkuk has some serious questions. "O Lord, how long shall I cry, and thou wilt not hear? ... Why dost thou shew me iniquity, and cause me to behold grievance? ... the law is slacked, and judgment doth never go forth; for the wicked doth compass about the righteous; therefore wrong judgment proceedeth." (1:2-4). Allow me to paraphrase, "Why, God, are You letting things go so long and get so bad without doing anything?" God answers, "Behold —I will work a work in your days, which ye will not believe, though it be told you—. I raise up the Chaldeans, that bitter and hasty nation, which shall march through the breadth of the land, to possess the dwelling places that are not theirs. They are terrible and dreadful; ... they shall come all for violence—he shall pass over, and offend, imputing this his power unto his god" (1:5-11). Basically God answered Habakkuk's question with, "I am going to do something. My plan is already in place and on the way. I am going to bring an evil army across the nation that will loot and kill and destroy. He will then add insult to injury by setting up idols and worship centers to his false god and give him the credit." This answer so stunned the prophet that he got very quiet and cautious and said, "I will stand upon my watch, and set me upon the tower, and will watch to see what he will say unto me, and what I shall answer when I am reproved" (2:1). He did the right thing. His questioning turned to listening. His pacing turned to standing still. His way forward was to stop. **Sometimes the best movement of faith is to not move at all and yet believe in the character of God.** One time I was invited to take over a very troubled ministry. After a short assessment, I told the leadership, "We must call this ministry to a complete stop." Basically I was giving them permission to rest from striving and trying to make things happen.

Back to our friend Habakkuk – Patrick Morley says it best. "There was the God that Habakkuk wanted and there was the God that was, and they were not the same." Often in our ministries, God doesn't seem to behave as we would like. Our call is still to believe. In fact, if I could condense this chapter into one sentence, it would be this: **when God can't be understood, He can be embraced by faith and that makes Him very happy.** Habakkuk's name means "one who embraces". We must do the same at times.

The healthy dialogue between the prophet and God yielded three answers from God that provide pillars for the faith of any believing servant of God during any conditions.

1. "— The just shall live by his faith" (2:4). This signature verse repeated three times in the New Testament lets us know that, if we are going to live with God, we are going to live by faith.

2. "— The earth shall be filled with the knowledge of the glory of the Lord, as the waters cover the sea" (2:14). Someday everybody will get it, and it doesn't all have to happen today or through us.

3. "— The Lord is in His holy temple; let all the earth keep silence before Him (2:20). In other words, "Be still, and know that I am God; I will be exalted among the heathen, I will be exalted in the earth. The Lord of hosts is with us; the God of Jacob is our refuge." Selah (Psalm 46:10, 11).

God knows we are in ministry, and He is as pleased with our believing heart as He is with our working hands. You may have to say to some of the anxious folks around, "This is a time for us to stand still, be still, and listen." Give them permission to only believe.

Through this experience, Habakkuk came out with a new song – one written from a real life experience. Here are the lyrics:

Habakkuk's Song

Although the fig tree shall not blossom,
Neither shall fruit be in the vines;
The labour of the olive shall fail,
And the fields shall yield no meat;
The flock shall be cut off from the fold,
And there shall be no herd in the stalls;
Yet I will rejoice in the Lord,
I will joy in the God of my salvation.
The Lord God is my strength,
And He will make my feet like hinds' feet,
And He will make me to walk upon
Mine high places. –Habakkuk 3:17-19

> *Jesus considers our faith in Him to be our greatest calling and priority work.*

So after some great movements of grace when expectations soar, don't be surprised if the landscape looks bleak. Remember, if God can't be understood, He can be embraced by faith. And if you will lay down any pride and believe the best is yet to come because the Lord is in His holy temple, you too may sing a new song and tell a new story of faith which only brings more grace.

Finally, Jesus Himself gives us instruction to let faith in Him be our first and primary work. In John 6, we find Jesus being pursued by the multitudes. He knew they were only "bread and fish" followers and told them so when He said, "Ye seek Me, not because ye saw the miracles, but because ye did eat of the loaves, and were filled." He then challenged their values by saying, "Labour not for the meat which perisheth, but for that meat which endureth unto everlasting life — " (v. 27). They responded with this question, "What shall we do, that we might work the work of God?" (v. 28). Jesus answered, "This is the work of God, that ye believe on Him whom He hath sent" (v. 29).

Jesus considers our faith in Him to be our greatest calling and priority work. Everything flows from that. He loves it when we really believe that what we believe is really real. In ministry, if we are going to live with God, we are going to live by faith. Paul said, "For in Jesus Christ neither circumcision availeth anything nor uncircumcision but faith which works by love." (Gal. 5:6). When the stewardship of faith becomes the lifestyle of our church, there will be a growing core of believers who discover Him to not only be their salvation but also their sufficiency and satisfaction. They will walk in revival, ready to continue in worship.

21

In Worship

"—Worthy is the Lamb that was slain to
Receive power, and riches, and wisdom,
And strength, and honour, and glory,
And blessing,
—Blessing, and honour,
And glory, and power, be unto Him
That sitteth upon the Throne, and unto
The Lamb for ever and ever —" –Revelation 5:12, 13

The life and authority of Christ continues by regular acts of worship. – (The Stewardship of Worship)

<u>Our Stewardship:</u> To maintain a first love relationship with Jesus through Scripture-based adoration.

<u>Action:</u> Constantly remind the flock that worship is a lifestyle where we do all things for an audience of ONE. This simple yet powerful approach was perfectly modeled by Jesus Himself.

This chapter is only meant to discuss the subject of worship as it relates to the church's first-love relationship with Jesus. All churches begin to lose the power of grace through faith when they leave their first love. A reviving brings new life, new life leads to new ministries, new ministries lead to new busy schedules, new initiatives, new ideas, new standards and with good intent we leave town without Jesus. He gets lost because of the company. (Luke 2:44). The reality of church life is that we will always find ourselves fighting for first love. Our ministries will not drift into first love. Even a "purpose-driven" church must be very careful to assure that love for Jesus drives our intentions. **Sometimes our ambition can become our worst enemy, especially if the Lord graces us with bountiful resources.**

The Ephesian church had enjoyed great grace from God. The apostle Paul, along with Timothy and the apostle John, had started the church at Ephesus. Paul was greatly by the church there. When he was about to leave after reporting to them for the last time, they hugged him and kissed him and cried because he said he would never see them again (Acts 20:36-38).

The Lord Jesus, the Head of the church, gives His assessment of this great church.

> *"I know thy works, and thy labour, and thy*
> *Patience, and how thou canst not bear*
> *Them which are evil; and thou hast tried*
> *Them which say they are apostles, and are*
> *Not, and hast found them liars; and hast*
> *Borne, and hast patience, and for my*
> *Name's sake hast labored, and hast not*
> *Fainted."* –Revelation 2:2,3

These were a suffering people who were patient, hated evil, tried false apostles, persevered, worked hard without quitting for Jesus' name. From the outside, they looked almost perfect. But Jesus knew their hearts were growing cold toward Him and described them as having left their first love. Something we need to remember here is that when our love for Jesus grows cool, so does our love for each other. If we are honest, we have to admit that Jesus is easier

Our ambition can become our worst enemy.

to love than people. Often we fail to recognize that the compromised ministry and outreach of our church started with our interrupted love for Jesus.

Jesus, with His omnisciently accurate assessment, faithfully reveals to the Ephesian church their problems, then tells them what to do about it.

> *"Nevertheless I have somewhat against thee,*
> *Because thou hast left thy first love.*
> *Remember therefore from whence thou art*
> *Fallen, and repent, and do the first works;*
> *Or else I will come unto thee quickly, and will*
> *Remove thy candlestick out of his place, except*
> *Thou repent."* –Revelation 2:4, 5

He gives them a divinely solemn ultimatum. They could remember, repent, and return their hearts to Him, or He would remove their candlestick! That's scary! While we might excuse a cold heart for Jesus as an "acceptable sin," He sees it as a reason to close a church down!

Here are some general observations:

1. A church can appear to be doing everything right and still be in trouble.
2. Leaving our first love is a sin and grieves Jesus.
3. Leaving our first love can lead to the removal of our witness as a church.
4. We can listen, change, and be blessed.

> "He that hath an ear let him hear
> What the Spirit saith unto
> The churches; to Him that
> Overcometh will I give to eat of
> The tree of life, which is in the
> Midst of the paradise of God." –Revelation 2:7

5. The Lord Himself knows all the intimate details. This should always be a great comfort to any leader. It should also be a call to prayer.

This raises two major questions in my mind. What is first love, and what are first works?

Anything I've ever read or heard on the subject of first love related it to the way someone may have felt when they were first saved. Early on they had the joy of being forgiven, the relief of escaping eternal damnation, the hope of a new beginning, in other words, a clean slate. A combination of these provided somewhat of a spiritual honeymoon, which for some reason, cooled over time. So the idea I had before was that I needed to go back to those early feelings when I first fell in love with Jesus. That idea doesn't work for me for several reasons.

1. Feelings can't drive the spiritual train. The fact of Scriptural truth must inform our spirits which then encourages our hearts in love toward Jesus.

2. Feelings were not a major part in my conversion. It was more of a surrender of the will to Him!

3. I love Jesus more today than I ever have. I don't want to go back. In fact, if done right, the Christian life centered in God's Word and understanding should cause our love for Jesus to increase over time. Growing in grace and knowledge is a treasure that constantly awards unending dividends.

So what is first love? Here's my definition.

First love happens when we find in another what is desperately needed in ourselves. And the greater the desperation, the greater the appreciation and adoration. There is no greater demonstration of this than the scene at the cross. It was a showdown. Three major doctrinal realties converge at the cross.

1. The holiness of God accompanied with all of its perfect justice, its all-consuming fire and wrath.

2. The total depravity of man accompanied with its clear demonstration of rebellion and ignorance.

> "*First love*" *happens when we find in another what is desperately needed in ourselves.*

3. The unconditional love, mercy, and forgiveness of God as His innocent Lamb is willingly caught in the thicket for us!

Fast forward to the most vulnerable day of our lives when we will stand before His holiness. What will our "felt-need" be? It will be to be robed in the righteousness of Jesus. We believers will spontaneously worship in appreciation throughout eternity with an attitude of first love knowing first-hand how desperate we really were. That desperation needs to be studied in the Scriptures, reviewed in our fellowship, and demonstrated in our lifestyle of worship.

What are First Works?

A picture is worth a thousand words, so the scene I would like to relate here is that of the sinner woman who crushed the Pharisee's arrogance when he invited Jesus to dinner (Luke 7:36-50). Twice Luke relates in the narrative that she was a noted sinner. Her worship was described as follows: "And, behold, a woman in the city, which was a sinner, when she knew that Jesus sat at meat in the Pharisee's house, brought an alabaster box of ointment, and stood at His feet behind Him weeping, and began to wash His feet with tears, and did wipe them with the hairs of her head, and kissed His feet, and anointed them with the ointment" (v. 37, 38).

Luke's description of her actions and the intensity of the verbs used here lets us know that <u>she made a scene</u> to express her desperate need and loving appreciation. As leaders we must cultivate this kind of worship as the lifestyle of our church.

Expressions may vary, but our hearts should be hot with love.

The gospel is good news for bad people.

Jesus observed the bewilderment of the Pharisee and engaged him in a dialogue in which He explained the difference between the Pharisee's lack of respect for Jesus and the sinner woman's lavish gestures, i.e., the Pharisees rationalizing his deep need of forgiveness while the sinful woman seemingly recognized her need for forgiveness. Jesus summarized His analysis of the situation with this, "To whom little is forgiven, the same loveth little" (v. 47). A good servant-leader is always reminding himself and those he leads of how much they have been forgiven. From this story, I would suggest that the first worksJesus seeks in believers is a heart condition that reflects our deep need of Him in the light of the blazing holiness of God and the <u>relief</u> believers experience having learned that Jesus paid it all. My heart leaps afresh as I write this. Roy Hession says, **"The gospel is good news for bad people."** That should make us worship and turn every act of service into a sweet gesture of thanksgiving. From the example of this woman, let me suggest three practices that may partially describe the place to which Jesus would like us to return.

1. Honest, humble repentance. The Lord sees repenters as those who worship Him with the ongoing admission of their need.
2. Demonstrative faith. The Lord sees believers as those who worship Him with ongoing trust in Christ as their only hope.
3. Extravagant thanksgiving. The Lord sees givers as those who take every opportunity to worship with obedient acts of service and sacrifice as an ongoing expression of gratefulness. They have moved from dead works of obligation to the fragrance of adoration.

If we are going to cooperate with Jesus as He fills the church with His life, we must teach our people this style of worship. This is the heart of worship, and it goes much deeper than the emotions we experience over a favorite style of music.

Revelation Chapter 5 puts this entire idea in context where we see God on the throne with the title deed of the universe in His right hand. He instructs a strong angel to ask a question that paralyzes everyone.

"Who is worthy to open the book, and loose the seals thereof?" (v. 2) No one spoke; no one was able to open the book or even look at it. John wept much as everyone stood silent with shamed faces. One elder broke the silence, comforted their hearts, and introduced Jesus by calling him The Lion of the tribe of Judah, the Root of David, who hath prevailed to open the book, and to loose the seven seals thereof. The "Slain Lamb" appeared in the middle of the throne and took the book so that God's plan for the ages could move forward. If we let our biblical imagination work here, we realize this is a breath-taking moment. At that point, everyone celestial and everyone terrestrial yet redeemed begins to worship. New songs of worthiness and redemption burst forth.

"Worthy is the Lamb that was slain to receive power, and riches, and wisdom, and strength, and honour, and glory, and blessing" (v. 12). This is the perfect revelation of the first-love worship of the sufficiency of Christ, and we must do our best to imitate it in our churches. If this scene of heavenly beings reveals such thankfulness, how much more should we on earth feel the need to respond in like manner?

How do we lead our congregations to revive and maintain their first love? By reminding ourselves of the ongoing intentional focus on the person and cross-work of Jesus Christ. Jesus Himself gave the church a way to do this when He instituted the Lord's Supper.

"And He took bread, and gave thanks, and brake it,
And gave unto them saying, 'This is My body which
Is given for you; this do in remembrance of Me.
Likewise also the cup after supper, saying, This cup
Is the New Testament in My blood, which is shed for you."
–Luke 22:19,20

The Lord knows how prone we are to forget the gravity of our lostness and the sacrifice for our salvation, so He built in a simple yet significant way for us to be reminded. I have found the more intense church life becomes, the more frequent the Lord's Supper should be practiced.

At times it should be made the priority of the day, the center piece of the worship event. When Paul reviews this with the Corinthian church, he emphasizes the word "remembrance." He also clearly states that, "as often as ye eat this bread, and drink this cup, ye do shew the Lord's death till He come (I Cor. 11:26). He knew that the best way to remember was to review again and again until Jesus returns.

He also spoke of the attitudes to be displayed during this time of remembrance. Respectfulness, self-examination, reverence, fear of God, and discernment all create a sacred biblical moment as we pause in quietness remembering the Lamb at Calvary. Make these moments a priority as often as you are led. An intentional review of the past can help sanctify the present and set us on course for future ministry. These are times when you as a leader can call your ministry to a stop and give everyone a chance to tell Jesus of their love. Your people are constantly fighting the rush of the everyday and will benefit greatly from these sacred breaks. Give your congregation "Selah" moments for remembrance and reflection. You may have to trim your message and cut some music, but the benefits will protect you from Jesus coming and shutting the ministry down completely! We have authority through Jesus to defeat the attacks of Satan, but when Jesus sets His face against us, we will be gone (Rev. 2:5).

In summary, the loving worship of Jesus can never be separate from the understanding of Scripture. The Bible does allow us to have objective truth (logos) and subjective reality (rhema) but we will never enjoy first-love in our spirits without the Word of God.

When Jesus met the woman at the well (John 4), He said to her that the Father was seeking true worshipers. In His dialogue with her, He exposed three categories of worshipers (4:22, 23):

1. Ignorant worshipers. "Ye worship ye know not what."
2. Knowledgeable worshipers. "We know what we worship."
3. True worshipers. "But the hour cometh and now is, when the true worshipers shall worship the Father in spirit and in truth."

That's our goal. In this stewardship, we must lead our flock to become true worshipers who love Jesus through obedience and adoration. We are then ready to face adversity in warfare.

22

In Warfare

"Finally, my brethren, be strong in the Lord,
And the power of His might." –Ephesians 6:10

"Thou therefore, my son, be strong in the
Grace that is in Christ Jesus." –II Timothy 2:1

The authority/sufficiency of Christ is tried and
proven in the oven of adversity.
–(The Stewardship of Adversity)

Our Stewardship: To fight (agonize) the good fight
of faith. –I Timothy 6:12

This verse from Paul's instruction to young Timothy was used in
both military and athletic endeavors to describe the concentration,
discipline, and extreme effort needed to win. The "good fight of faith"
is the spiritual conflict with Satan's kingdom of darkness in which all
men of God are necessarily involved. We do not wrestle against flesh
and blood (Eph. 6:12); we do not war according to the flesh
(II Cor. 10:3), and our weapons of warfare are not carnal (human) but
mighty in God for pulling down strongholds (II Cor. 10:4). In a word,
the Bible clearly says, our enemies are not flesh, our war is not a flesh-
effort, and our weapons are not human! But when our church is
fighting, all we encounter seems to be flesh! We read body language,
see angry faces, hear cutting words and watch the hallway huddles that

curb their conversation when we walk near. All these signs of flesh give us suspicions about the war with the darkness.

A good steward of revival must not be surprised when adversity comes.

This chapter is the main reason this book is being written. Let me say it simply and clearly, **A good steward of revival must not be surprised when adversity comes.** Adversity is as much a part of life with the Vine as grace and faith and worship. Many a church has been caught off guard, discouraged, disillusioned, and defeated because they thought the reviving of God was a cure-all – the end of all problems. To this day I am confronted by those who discredit the revival in our region in 1985 and even blame the revival as the beginning of church problems! Remember also that trials come from without and from within. The ones from within are the most hurtful and surprising.

Peter helps us here. *"Beloved, think it not strange concerning the fiery trial which is to try you, as though some strange thing happened unto you;"* (I Peter 4:12)

In seamless fashion he continues to equip the believer with six attitudes that will enable him to endure and employ the fire.

1. Expect it (v. 12)
2. Rejoice in it (v. 13,14)
3. Evaluate the cause (v. 15-18)
4. Entrust it to God (v. 19)
5. Feed the flock with truth (5:2)
6. Take oversight willingly (5:2)

You must lead your flock to do the same. Fighting each other is not an option. **Remaining objective when under fire is one of the toughest challenges of ministry.**

Don't fight alone. "Two are always better than one," and "a threefold cord is not quickly broken" (Eccl. 4:9-12).

A pastor should always be in the process of enlarging his intimate prayer team and building a team-type ministry. There is a reason why Jesus sent the 70 out 2x2, why He called Paul *and* Barnabas and why Paul only traveled alone once. Paul's missionary journeys were, for the most part, a team effort. In a multitude of counselors, there is safety (Prov. 15:22; 24:6).

Remaining objective when under fire is one of the toughest challenges of ministry.

Ellen S. Lister selected quotes from the letters of Samuel Rutherford (1600-1661) and put them together in a tiny book entitled *The Loveliness of Christ.* Many of his letters were an encouragement to ministers who were suffering adversity. These two quotes are helpful to us here.

"I found it most true, that the greatest temptation out of hell is to live without temptation; Grace withereth without adversity. The devil is but God's master fencer, to teach us to handle our weapons."

A reviving from God is not the end of all battles but rather an equipping for battles. The sovereign working of God in revival will prepare us for the sovereignly approved visitation of trials. That's why stewardship of adversity is so important. God is not about protecting us from all warfare but rather providing us with mighty weapons for warfare.

Rutherford's second quote introduces another dimension of adversity that is often overlooked, i.e., the ways of God.

"My shallow and ebb thoughts are not the compass Christ saileth by. I leave His ways to Himself, for they are far, far above me. There are windings and to's and fro's in His ways, which blind bodies like us cannot see." Dear friend, please remember we are living with the vibrant, lovely and life-giving Vine whose ways are past finding out (Rom. 11:33). Don't be surprised by the windings, the reverses, or the quietness. My friend Andy Harkleroad reminds us, "The Teacher is silent during the test but He is not absent." He is building His church even when we can't imagine it.

When hard times come, we often forget the splendor of God's ways. He knows that grace grows best in winter. Isaiah captured it in classic fashion.

> "For My thoughts are not your thoughts,
> Neither are your ways My ways, saith the Lord.
> For as the heavens are higher than the earth,
> So are My ways higher than your ways, and
> My thoughts your thoughts." –Isaiah 55:8, 9

My life changed in 1974 when I heard Bill Gothard teach about the ways of God. His instruction at that time was for us to note this sequence in Scripture.

1. God starts with a vision followed by a
2. Death of a vision then possibly a
3. Double death of a vision then a
4. Supernatural fulfillment of the vision.

Abraham is a model of this. God's promise to Abraham being a great nation was followed by a barren womb which then produced the promised child in old age. All of our faith heroes experienced "death valley" days so that God would get all the glory.

The temptation for us during those days is to either quit or take matters into our own hands. Neither option is good stewardship. Abraham's choice to go into Hagar has left some serious side effects. **The point here is that your ministry may have to go backward before it goes forward.** When it does, don't defect and don't manipulate. This is a time to be still, be obedient, and let patience have her perfect work. Remember this is not a book about how to do it. Leading your flock responsibly through God-ordained adversity is an art learned at the hand of the Father. He is the faithful Husbandman of the vine-branch relationship. He knows how to purge and prop every branch for maximum fruit. While on a mission in Southern France, I was astonished at how brutally the vinedressers trimmed the vines in order to experience a greater harvest. Sometimes it's extremely hard to know what's going on. But don't panic. Just stay faithful.

Here's a faith-cycle you may notice in your ministry. Turbulent winds, if responded to properly, can help our lives and ministries to soar higher. It's like setting our sail to catch the wind. It's like an eagle who soars higher because of the storm. Even the Wright Brothers remind us that "Birds don't soar in a calm."

Here's a common scenario of turbulence.

1. We experience a lack, threat, or need which causes —
2. An inner disturbance in which we —
3. Yield our will – we surrender to God
4. There is momentary affirmation
5. Followed by deeper despair calling for greater trust which is rewarded by (This could be that "double death of a vision")
6. An inner rest and inner supply which frees us to —
7. Analyze the situation
8. Birth a plan of action and
9. Take faith-sized steps

This cycle is evenly divided into three parts in which we choose (1-3), trust (4-6), and act (7-9). This is a very common cycle used by the faithful servants of Scripture. Moses, for instance, chose to suffer with the people of God. He trusted God with a long, rollercoaster-type of experience until he marched with 1.5 million people out of Egypt. We revere his endurance to the end as he lived out God's calling on his life. If you lead your ministry to ride the winds of turbulence, you will be a faithful steward.

This same pattern is seen in the Apostle Paul's first missionary journey. (Acts 13, 14). In Cyprus, Antioch and Iconium, the same sequence appears.

1. Communication
2. Opposition
3. Perseverance
4. Fruit
5. Glory

It should be comforting to us to know that this great steward of the mysteries of God (I Cor. 4:1) also faced great opposition in the process of being faithful. The writer of Hebrews reminds us that, if we find ourselves wearied and faint in our minds, we must fix our eyes on Jesus who endured the contradiction of sinners like no one else. Through perfect obedience, He earned the right to sit down at the right hand of the Throne of God.

Satan's Devices

This chapter has not offered much instruction in actual warfare tactics. Mostly I have written to remind you that adversity is always par for the course, especially when God is up to something great. Since we must not let Satan take advantage of us, we must not be ignorant of his devices (II Cor. 2:11). Here is a short list of his tactics I have found directly related to the subject of revival.

1. Expectations – Hope deferred makes the heart sick (Prov. 13:12a). Many will murmur like the Israelites did when their hidden expectations are not realized. They think a reviving is the end of all struggle. Lead them to place all expectations in Christ alone.

2. Ambition – A new surge of God's Spirit brings new life which births more ministry activity. This can quickly turn into selfish ambition and unnecessary busyness. Israel assumed Ai would fall like Jericho. Other things needed to be considered. Lead them to always stop and pray <u>first</u>.

3. Ignorance – People will be down on what they are not up on. Knowing how to set the sail to catch the wind of the Spirit is learned over time. Teach the Word and help them understand.

4. Extremes – A move of God's Spirit is often accompanied with extremes in behavior. Some are counterfeit; others are temporary emotional releases. Help them find reality in the Word and in normal life. If we seek the supernatural only in the sensational, we will miss the Holy Spirit.

5. Experience – There is often a special grace that accompanies a refreshing which is often interpreted as feelings. Warn them not to base faith on feelings but rather on the facts of Scripture. Also pray for them to have the spirit of revelation as they read the Scripture for themselves – Paul did (Eph. 1:15-22). They need inner sight.

6. Comparison – Often folks are tempted to compare the atmosphere during a reviving with that which is more long term. Sadly, there is always the ever-present spirit of the Pharisees who are sure they "have it" and others don't. This can create division. Let them know that we never arrive but must join hands and hearts and press on in obedience. Comparison is very unwise (II Cor. 10:12).

7. Revival – I know it seems odd for me to mention revival itself as a tactic of Satan. The point here is that anything – anything – that takes center stage other than Jesus can be a distraction. I have noticed at times that people can get so excited about the effects of the workings of God that they forget about the God of the workings. Spurgeon said, "I needed peace. So I sought the Lord for peace. Then the dove of peace flew in my heart. I looked down at the dove and he flew away." Lead your flock back to the heart of worship. Remember that revival is **Jesus Christ** obviously present and actively in charge.

Stay alert to these sneaky devices and be safe.

Let me close this chapter with a Scripture that will launch us into our next stewardship. God is working through adversity in order to do you, as a leader, a favor. Listen to this from Paul, "— I hear that there be divisions among you; and I partly believe it. For there must be also heresies among you, that they which are approved may be made manifest among you" (I Cor. 11:18, 19).

Factions and adversity often reveal those who have passed the test of spiritual genuiness and purity. We will not be able to take the mixed multitude to maturity. Curious onlookers and "bread and fish" followers do not make the cut during adversity. Through trials, the cream rises to the top and the faithful remnant will appear. Honestly, I have often been surprised at who endures through hard times. Again, in the ministry of Jesus, "Many of His disciples went back, and walked no more with Him after some hard teachings" (John 6:66). From that time, many of His disciples went back and walked no more with Him. The residual effect of a faithful stewardship during adversity will leave you with a committed remnant who will then follow Jesus by choice.

23
Through Discipleship

"And the things that thou hast heard of
Me among many witnesses, the same
Commit thou to faithful men, who shall
*Be able to teach others also." –*II Timothy 2:2

The authority/reality of Christ becomes clearly focused when we count the cost and make a choice.

Our Stewardship: To disciple the faithful who will teach others.

By grace, through faith, in worship and in warfare, you should now begin to identify those who are being faithful in attitude and actions. They are to be discipled, trained, and commissioned. This is where we begin to multiply shepherds. When I started in ministry, discipleship was not emphasized, but I had a sense that new converts needed to be followed up. In a short time, there was not enough of "me" to go around. I started discipling in random manner just to survive. Now it's my way of life for ministry, and I find it delightful to watch the multiplication process take place. Making disciples is not a cookie-cutter process. Some grow faster than others. Different backgrounds will require varying approaches, etc., but the principle is the same. Train the faithful in ministry that is suited for their personality and calling. **If your ministry is to stay healthy while you grow in numbers then you must grow in good shepherds amongst the flock.**

Any reviving can experience some fall out which can be discouraging to you and disheartening to those who watch. The timid ones as well as the skeptics

If your ministry is to stay healthy while you grow in numbers then you must grow in good shepherds amongst the flock.

may try to discredit what God is doing, but you can be strong in grace and commit to the faithful your philosophy and approach to ministry. Their growth and passion will be a securing factor for the long haul and lay to rest the fear of others. For the most part, I have found that the net result of revival in a local ministry is a faithful remnant who have had their awareness of the crucified life and the filling of the Spirit raised. They have counted the cost and made the choice to follow Jesus at any cost. With no hidden expectations, no personal agenda, and no double-mindedness, they follow. They are rewarded with a growing reality in their relationship with Him which only serves to cause them to hunger for more. These deserve our priority attention. For years, I tried to keep the unfaithful in church while neglecting those faithful ones who always stayed by the Lord. **Multiply the faithful and you will multiply your ministry.**

There are many good resources today on how to do discipleship. You can research them and decide what approach best fits your situation. Just know that it's God's instruction to us and then get at it. Dr. Bob Jones Sr. said, "You can borrow brains but you can't borrow character." So borrow some great brains and go for it. There is no perfect, end-all method. Start doing life together and talk as you go along. Hands-on training coupled with Bible examination are great at any level, and there are many levels. Some disciples can hardly unpack John 3:16 while others are well advanced in information but simply lacking in application. You will have to sort out where you start and stop with each one. Don't be afraid to get dirty and don't be intimidated by those smarter than you. A great teacher makes the student think he knows more than the teacher.

Older to Younger

Don't forget that older teaching the younger is a very natural and effective way of commissioning the faithful and multiplying shepherds. Older, Spirit-filled believers who have weathered the storm of life make tremendous mentors. With the breakdown of the family, these folks provide surrogate dads and moms for the young who are raising their children. My dad's advice to me has paid immeasurable dividends in ministry. He told me again and again, "Joe, respect your elders. You will be old someday." I have heeded his advice, which is Scriptural, and have treated the older men as fathers and the older women as mothers. They have not only encouraged my life and family but have participated in ministry as well. It is my practice to give value to all ages which, in turn, opens their hearts to learning and growing. With this attitude on your part, you will discover the wisdom of the sage who has the freshness of youth. The key is discerning Spirit-filledness.

Paul was very bold to make this idea of the older teaching the younger a part of sound doctrine as well as a practical training dynamic which protects the Word of God from being blasphemed (Titus 2:1-5). The reviving life of Christ is well-served by these aging friends. This encouragement goes far deeper than slapping backs and goofy cliché talk. This is wisdom with skin on reaching out in loving relationships. Your discipleship role here is to help each one identify the gifts he or she owns that will well serve the younger part of the flock. This will give them dignity and fresh purpose. You may have to craft a ministry vehicle to get them started.

The Cost of Discipleship

Jesus defines the cost of discipleship clearly in Luke 14. Here's a summary of how he describes the attitude of those who are making the choices to let Jesus be the primary focus for their lives.

1. They have relinquished the right to have any relationship in their lives which they cherish more than their relationship with Jesus (v. 26). They are satisfied with Jesus.

2. They have relinquished the right to eliminate circumstances from their lives that make them uncomfortable (v. 27) They love not their lives unto death.

3. They have relinquished the ownership of the things which they possess (v. 33). They replace ownership with stewardship.

They who are carriers of this attitude are both fragrant and refreshing (Psalm 133). These are the effectual ministers of Christ's reviving life in your congregation. Your stewardship is to equip and resource them so that the life in them will permeate the body.

In this same passage, Jesus relates the evidences which appear when followers of Jesus are not surrendered in one or more of these areas:

1. Unfinished Projects (Luke 14:28-30)
   (Tower – Unfinished)
2. Premature Surrenders (Luke 14:31, 32)
   (Quitting before the enemy arrives)
3. Ineffective Testimony (Luke 14:34, 35)
   (Salt has lost its savor)

Obviously Jesus knew that many would fall into these categories. Don't write off those who fail to follow through completely. Be kind to them and include them as much as possible even though you may not be able to intensely work with them. Remember, they belong to God and what He began in them He is able to complete (Phil. 1:6). Some may come around later. Remember, God's timing is not always ours.

Live in a Discipleship Sandwich

Teach your congregation to live in a II Timothy 2:2 sandwich like Timothy. He was to be accountable to Paul and responsible for faithful men. If everyone will align themselves under a faithful person to whom they are accountable and pray to find God's person for whom they are responsible, disciples will multiply exponentially. I love to watch it happen.

The Road from Saul to Paul

It may help us to observe the Lord's sanctification process as He transformed Saul the terrorist into Paul the evangelist and church planter. It was not a straight line, nor a gentle slope upward. Every discipleship effort has some surprises. Notice these classic stages in Paul's life on the road to becoming God's apostle to the Gentiles. (Acts 9-13).

Stage 1 – Repentance and Faith (9:1-17). First there is a changed life. Repentance and faith are two sides of the same coin, and they both become the lifestyle of the Kingdom. **Someone who is not willing to change cannot be discipled.** The way people are brought in to the kingdom will make a difference in the Kingdom growth. Mental assent to the gospel without a work of the Spirit that convicts and regenerates will not last. Baptism is the first test of a disciple's motives. The baptism commitment to teach them to observe all things Jesus commanded needs to be a strong element in this stage (Matt. 28:18-20). Carefulness here will also aid in protecting your congregation from filling up with goats instead of sheep and tares instead of wheat, thus weakening the power of Christ's Spirit by the presence of unregenerate church members.

The Lord assured Ananias that Saul was genuine with the words, "Behold he prayeth" (v. 11). Desperate, humble praying is always a good sign of repentance. Ananias was skeptical of the conversion because of Saul's reputation of havoc. He was instructed by the Lord to give strong counsel in this early stage when Saul was chosen (v. 15) to bear the name of the Lord before the Gentiles and kings, as well as to Israel while suffering great things in the process! (v. 16) Wow! This is not your normal fresh start with Jesus material. I will say there is some advantage to knowing the tough stuff up front.

It's ok to let your disciples wrestle with the cost of following. Too much comfort too soon may stunt their growth.

Stage 2 – Enlightenment (Acts 9:17, 18). This is where the disciple learns about the One who made the change. Paul learned this so well up front, he was able to boldly say throughout his ministry, "For I am not ashamed of the gospel of Christ; for it is the power of God unto salvation to every one that believeth; to the Jew first, and also to the Greek" (Rom. 1:16). Only a Christ-centered gospel has the dynamite power to transform. The power of the gospel and the power of any reviving is one and the same, the surge of reformation teaching in our day is a move back to one power – the power of the resurrection of Christ. The eyes of our understanding need to be enlightened early to this mighty power which God worked in Christ toward us. How often legalism, formalism, and conformity to preference can subtly replace resurrection. Who is the Jesus of Scripture? Make it clear. Keep it clear. This became the single theme of Paul's life. "For to me to live is Christ —" (Phil. 1:21).

Stage 3 – Ministry Training (Acts 9:19, 20). This is basic involvement when the disciple observes and participates in a limited way with others in Kingdom work. Various servant roles provide a good entry level for learning. Don't give too much too soon and don't promote too quickly. Saul was with the disciples, and he did preach that Jesus was the Son of God. He was smitten with this reality and began declaring it immediately. Once a disciple knows the Lord and makes repenting his lifestyle, there will be a natural desire to get involved in ministry. When a disciple seeks you out and initiates ideas for involvement, you are well on your way to further development.

Don't mistake aggressive personalities for spiritual growth. Some may come to us with an orderly home, a balanced budget, personality, plus natural leadership qualities and executive training. We salivate at the possibilities of their presence in our ministries. Don't be afraid – be wise. They are still novices to the things of the Kingdom. Without meekness, this power-house of a person could become a Diotrephes who loves pre-eminence instead of a Demetrius who has a good report of all men and of the truth itself (III John). On the other hand, I have been so blessed by men and women of this caliber who came to Christ, were filled with the Spirit, lived at the cross, and brought to our ministry the tools of their marketplace experience which facilitated the gospel of the kingdom. They have refreshed me often. I love them.

Stage 4 – Leadership Development (Acts 9:21, 22). During this stage, participation in ministry becomes consistent, and leadership qualities and giftedness begin to surface. People around them begin to comment on the difference. This was especially true in Saul's case (v. 21). Saul increased in strength and his conviction about Christ coupled with his reasoning mind made him a ready defender, confounding the Jews and proving that Jesus was the Christ. This was happening without a lot of coaching from others. A good point to be made here is that when people are truly convicted by God, saved by God, are counting the cost of following God, and are hearing from God, they will increase with the fullness of God (Eph. 3:19). They are a joy to watch. Love, encourage, and protect them because the next stage may not be so easy.

Stage 5 – Separation and Re-evaluation (Acts 9:23-31). Leadership in God's work demands time and testing to prove authenticity and breaking of the vessel. The making of a minister is similar to the making of a ministry. Both are branch-like, abiding in the Vine, to be purged by the husbandman Father (John 15:2). Saul was a "hot potato" and needed some time to find his balance. The Jews were trying to kill him, and the disciples were afraid of him. Barnabas became his advocate before the apostles. While with the apostles in Jerusalem, he began disputing against the Grecians who in turn tried to slay him. The brethren finally brought him down to Caesarea and sent him forth to Tarsus. At this point, Paul disappeared from prominent ministry for several years, although he possibly founded some churches around Syria and Cilicia (Gal. 1:21).

Depending on the circumstances, **God knows how to move His disciples around for their ongoing growth and refinement.** Don't be surprised if some of your most prized disciples will be moved by God in some way or face unexpected changes. Don't be discouraged. The Potter knows what each vessel needs. Each vessel needs space to count the cost and make a choice. Numerous times through my journey with hardship and isolation, I knew that the next step would have to be by grace or there would be no step at all. How thankful I am today for those who opened their hands and helped me then remain faithful in prayer.

*T*he reward of disciple making is the call of God.

Stage 6 – Leadership in Ministry (Acts 11:25, 26). Here the leader leads. It is now time for the disciple-in-progress to practice the decisions he made in his time of testing. By now he can teach from both knowledge and experience. He now relates with the attitude of brokenness and dependence.

Through Peter's ministry to Cornelius in Acts 10, the Holy Spirit came to the Gentiles. When he reported to Jerusalem and rehearsed with them how "the Holy Spirit fell on them, as on us at the beginning" (Acts 11:15), they glorified God and admitted peacefully that God had granted repentance to the Gentiles. Now they needed an apostle to this new people group of the Gentiles. Guess what? They had one in storage! When the church in Jerusalem heard this, they sent Barnabas to Antioch (11:22), and he went from there to Tarsus to seek Saul and brought him back to serve in Antioch. Saul was now ready to serve in team ministry with others. The ministry was growing and healthy, and the disciples were given a new name – Christian. How blessed when the world sees Christ in our discipleship.

Stage 7 – World Vision (Acts 13:1-3). This is now a maturity that is open to God's sovereign placement. I love this moment described here. "As they ministered to the Lord, and fasted, the Holy Ghost said, 'Separate Me Barnabas and Saul for the work whereunto I have called them.' And when they had fasted and prayed, and laid their hands on them, they sent them away" (Acts 13:2, 3).

The reward of disciple-making is the call of God. Some are called to stay with us and some are called to go elsewhere. Either way, we are multiplying ministry and building His church. Steward well. Like the apostle Paul, growing disciples often get their start within the body.

24
Within the Body

"And He gave some, apostles; and some,
Prophets; and some evangelists; and
Some pastors and teachers, for the
Perfecting of the saints, for the work of
The ministry, for the edifying of the body
Of Christ:" –Ephesians 4:11, 12

The reality of Christ permeates the true church as the body ministers to itself in love. –(The Stewardship of Body Life)

<u>Our Stewardship:</u> To equip the saints within the local body to live and serve in harmony and to edify one another in love. –Ephesians 4:16

The reviving life of the Vine thrives in an atmosphere of love where people are laying down their lives for their friends. Our job as shepherds is to equip them to minister to each other. This chapter is different from the previous one in that while discipleship is focused on the growth of the individual, this stewardship focuses on the health of the whole body.

I was introduced to the concept of equipping when I was 30, just prior to starting my relationship with our second church. Before that, I basically understood myself to be a preacher, teacher, soul winner, visitation pastor, and activity director. I was your typical one-man band. Again, it was all I knew. My beloved seminary professor and predecessor in our second church, Dr. Gerry Benn, shared this concept with me, and my ministry life took on a whole new adventure. The Bible says that the pastor is Christ's gift to the church to equip the saints for the work of ministry. I resisted this truth at first because I feared the delegation of ministry would be interpreted as laziness on my part. However, when our people saw the effect of many hands and felt the joy of ownership and my trust in them, they formed a great team to minister with intention. I like to think of it like coaching. Help each member to assess his or her gifts and callings, train him or her in how to use those gifts in the body, and then plug each individual into practical ministry within the body to serve one another. I suggest you familiarize yourself with the motivational gifts of Romans 12 and then lead members to identify which ones best describe their heart throb for ministry. Here's what each heart-gift might relate if you asked them what they were looking for in a church. I actually was taught these at the "Institute of Basic Life Principles" advanced seminar one year after I realized I needed to equip my flock. God has always provided just what I needed at just the right time.

Here's the list of gifts in order with their emphasis:

Prophets – Look for well-prepared sermons exposing sin, proclaiming righteousness, and warning of judgment to come.

Servers – Look for practical assistance to each member of the church to encourage him and to help him fulfill his responsibilities.

Teachers – Look for in-depth Bible studies with special emphasis on precise meaning of words.

Exhorters – Look for personal counseling and encouragement for each member to assist him in applying Scriptural principles to his daily living.

Givers – Look for generous programs of financial assistance to missionaries and other ministries.

Administrators – Look for smooth-running organizations throughout the church so that every phase will be carried out decently and in order.

Mercy Showers – Look for special outreach and concern for the precise and varying feelings of individuals with a readiness to meet their needs.

While an attitude of serving should prevail at all times, knowledge of specific giftedness and motivation helps the servant enjoy the journey more and bring maximum benefit to all. Warren Wiersbe says, **"Ministry happens when divine resources meet human needs through loving channels for the glory of God."** God is always the source, but loving channels properly placed are a God-send to the body. You can never be everything to everybody, but the body working together becomes the fullness of Christ in your midst. A good pastor learns how to distribute the gifts God has given. This stewardship of body life also relates to the first two stewardships of grace and faith.

Ministry happens when divine resources meet human needs through loving channels for the glory of God.

"For I say, through the grace given unto me, to every man that is among you, not to think of himself more highly than he ought to think, but to think soberly, according as God hath dealt to every man the measure of faith. For as we have many members in one body, and all members have not the same office: So we being many are one body in Christ, and every one members one of another" (Rom. 12:3-5).

Paul lists five qualitative goals that flow from a body that effectively edifies itself in love (Eph. 4:13-16).

1. Unity of the faith (v. 13a). This is a unity of confidence in the character of God as well as a unity in transforming gospel doctrine.

2. <u>Christlikeness of believers</u> (v. 13b). This is a church with members that are becoming like the Jesus. They are approaching the measure of the stature of the fullness of Christ.

3. <u>Stability of believers</u> (v. 14). These are Christians who know what they believe and why. We especially need this in our postmodern, post-Christian, subjective truth culture. Every worldview must be accountable for its own interpretation. When I started 50 years ago, the landscape of the culture looked quite different. Many of my younger disciples are actually coaching me in the changes in today's mindset – another example of the ministry of the body even to its pastor. Changing winds of doctrine should not blow us off course. **Revival thrives best where doctrinal stability secures the foundation.**

4. <u>Truthing in Love</u> (v. 15). This is a literal translation of the original. Speaking the truth in love is an indication of growing up into Christ, our Head. When our confidence in God is strong, Christlikeness dominates our attitude, and our doctrine is secure. It becomes us, then, to be able to speak the truth in love. Truthing in love serves the gospel well whether we are witnessing to the lost, correcting our children, or confronting our peers with sensitive issues. The life of the Vine flows freely through this quality of the branch.

5. <u>Harmony of the Body</u> (v. 16). Here we see that Christ makes the whole body fit together by flowing through each member as he or she does his or her part, thus helping other parts to grow so that the whole body is healthy and growing in full love.

Pastor, if you're like me, you would rejoice to see this happening in your church. At this point, equipping the saints for ministry should look pretty valuable to us.

The Heart Class

A right start with new members is strategic to their becoming team players who are fruitful branches. To facilitate getting off on the right foot, we have found an energetic, new members class as a highly effective prerequisite to joining the church. We call ours "The Heart Class." Obviously, you can choose your own name and schedule accordingly. The reason I chose that name is because I believe all meaningful relationships begin with the heart. These classes help new ones have a designated time with the pastor. It's my favorite thing to do in church ministry. If I am excited about our church ministry, then I want to introduce it to these new ones myself. I love fielding their questions and being open with them. One of the ways Satan likes to bring division to a church is through hidden expectations. This class gives me an opportunity to express where we really are as a church so their expectations will not be too high. It's better to start low and build than to create a mental image of your church which cannot be met.

Just between you and me, there are four key things I want to accomplish through this Heart Class effort.

1. I want them to know that Jesus is the heart of our church – not music, sports, children's ministry, grand productions, coffee bars, concerts, great speakers, etc. He must be our all in all.

2. I want them to know that we are a church on purpose. We may look random because of our limitations, but in the cockpit, we have a destination. Our purpose is "making disciples who make disciples." Everything is driven by that.

3. I want them to be saved. Many people have been saved through the Heart Class because we ask them to write out their testimony. I always offer help with this at whatever level is needed. We believe in regenerate church membership, and we do not do anyone a favor by letting them become members without salvation. I make this clear to them. You

may lose some at this point, but be kind and rest in the Lord. Satan would love to fill the church with goats instead of sheep and tares instead of wheat. For them to have their testimony in clear form is a great witnessing tool and a blessing to the family of God as well as the individual. Their story as it relates to the gospel is life giving.

4. I want them to know that the church is an organism and not an organization. Doctrine, goals and ministry strategies all flow from the written Word (Bible) and the Living Word, both of which are supernatural and are our only hope of transforming lives for the glory of God. What a privilege to be a part of this living, breathing, reproductive organism. It's a power, not a form. A vibrant well-planned Heart Class can serve to unite hearts around Christ from the beginning of our relationship.

Church Discipline

The practice of church discipline is necessary to keep the radical cells of false doctrine, immorality, and division from destroying the spiritual health of a local church. Many of us have had a brush with cancer. Cancer that overtakes a human body starts with a few radical cells that will *Church discipline will not work in an environment where relationships are not nurtured.* not submit to the headship of the organism and for various reasons will not flush away with the normal cleansing process of the body. They begin to have a life of their own. They organize, metastasize, and eventually go on the attack, destroying vital organs and then taking the life of the individual. We hate cancer, don't we? I also hate spiritual cancer. Through pride it sets out with a satanic agenda to destroy a local church. At this point, pastors, we need to follow Scripture and become spiritual surgeons.

Church discipline will not work in an environment where relationships are not nurtured. All discipline is most effective where people know they're loved. Rules without relationships breed rebellion. However, there is a sense of security when blatant sin is dealt with in an atmosphere of unconditional love. A study of Matthew 18:15-20 will explain to us Jesus' instructions on the matter. The subject is addressed in many of Paul's epistles as well. Mark Dever says, "Discipline helps the church that lives inside of the boundary line [of Scripture] stay true to the very things that are cause for drawing the line in the first place." This is a vital part of our stewardship.

"One Another"

The life of the Vine freely flows amongst the branches as we embrace our call and commitment to the "one another" commands of Scripture, both positive and negative. Don't overlook the Holy Spirit's curriculum for supernatural body life. Lead your flock to carefully consider the dynamic of each one as it is fleshed out in a real world. Imagine how a newcomer feels when he or she comes into an atmosphere where these are in place. Here's a sampling of them.

Romans 12:10 – "Be kindly affectionate one to another with
    brotherly love;
    In honour preferring one another."
    (God's way of giving significance and defending
    the gospel.)
Romans 12:16 – "Be of the same mind one to another."
    (God's way of developing fellowship.)
Romans 15:7 – "Wherefore receive ye one another, as Christ also
    received us to the glory of God."
    (God's way of showing acceptance.)

Romans 15:14 – "And I myself also am persuaded of you, my brethren, that ye also are full of goodness, filled with all knowledge, able also to admonish one another."
(Paul was encouraged that they could minister intelligently to one another.)

Galatians 5:13 – "For, brethren, ye have been called into liberty; only use not liberty for an occasion to the flesh, but by love serve one another."
(The freedom of liberty provides the energy to serve other believers.)

Galatians 6:1,2 – "Brethren, if a man be overtaken in a fault, ye which are spiritual, restore such an one in the spirit of meekness; considering thyself, lest thou also be tempted. Bear ye one another's burdens, and so fulfill the law of Christ."
(Here, even the restoration of a fallen brother is a team effort of body life.)

Ephesians 4:32 – "And be ye kind one to another, tenderhearted, forgiving one another, even as God for Christ's sake hath forgiven you."
(Kindness and forgiveness are major components to loving, long-term relationships.)

Hebrews 3:13 – "But exhort one another daily, while it is called Today; lest any of you be hardened through the deceitfulness of sin."
(The pastor doesn't have to be the only one who confronts and encourages.)

James 5:16 – "Confess your faults one to another, and pray one for another, that ye may be healed. The effectual fervent prayer of a righteous man availeth much."
(Healing physically and spiritually through honest confession before trusted friends and prayer breeds revival in the church.)

I Peter 4:9, 10 – "Use hospitality one to another without grudging. As every man hath received the gift, even so minister the same one to another, as good stewards of the manifold grace of God." (In a broken world, generosity ministered through hospitality gives a feeling of home and security to needy souls.)

Think of it. If these ten dynamics were functioning in our church through Spirit-filled believers, the reality of the life of Christ would be evident. In this context we model Jesus with skin on, incarnate! This kind of love draws true believers back to the assembly to enjoy the presence of Christ. The 1985 revival I experienced was characterized by this drawing, mostly because believers got honest about their own sins and were then free to lovingly minister to others. *The assembly of "freed up" believers is unselfish and contagious.* This is a worthy stewardship for any pastor to teach, train, and model. Through this, he can enjoy ongoing revival within the body which breaks forth into the world.

The Life of the Vine in the Soul of the Church – 7 Stewardships of Revival

25
Into the World

"And they, continuing daily with one accord in the temple,
and breaking bread from house to house, did eat their
meat with gladness and singleness of heart, praising God,
and having favour with all the people. And the Lord
added to the church daily such as should be saved."

–Acts 2:46, 47

The good news of the resurrected life of Christ
penetrates the darkness of the lost world when the
church overflows with the witness and gladness of
God's grace. –(The Stewardship of Evangelism)

Help Their Joy

How often I heard Ralph and Lou Sutera say, "When revival is the
experience of the church, then evangelism will be the expression of the
church." Del Fehsenfeld said the same thing from a different direction.
"Some believers wouldn't wish their Christianity on their worst enemy."
In agreement, John Piper says, "People who prize Jesus praise Jesus." He
continues, "Missions exist because worship doesn't." Nehemiah of old
said to his workers, "The joy of the Lord is your strength." (Neh. 8:10).
One of my favorite messages during our Sutera ministry was entitled,
"Joy is the serious business of heaven." The Psalmist queried, "Wilt thou
be angry with us forever? Wilt thou draw out thine anger to all
generations? Wilt thou not revive us again, that thy people may rejoice
in thee?" (Psalm 85:5, 6).

Our stewardship of shepherding here should result in the saints enjoying such reality in Christ that they minister out of the overflow of a full heart. I realize that life is not always "happy, happy, happy." But we are instructed to "Let the Word of Christ dwell in you richly in all wisdom; teaching and admonishing one another in psalms and hymns and spiritual songs, singing with grace in your hearts to the Lord" (Col. 3:16). An essential part of the witness of our lives in and out of the church is joy. I love to say that singing is not for those who have a voice but for those who have a song. **We who serve or lead should not go very long without our song.** Sheep feel secure with a joyful shepherd whose habit is only to be angry with the wolves. Paul related his heart to the problem-ridden church at Corinth. "Moreover I call God for a record upon my soul, that to spare you I came not as yet unto Corinth. Not for that we have dominion over your faith, but helpers of your joy; for by faith ye stand" (II Cor. 1:23, 24). With God as witness, Paul said:

Joy is the serious business of heaven.

Sheep feel secure with joyful shepherds.

1. I gave you time and space to repent.
2. I have no interest in domination.
3. I am a helper of your joy.

In this stewardship of evangelism, we are right to start with being helpers and models of joy. Countless times over these 50 years, I have had to find a place to retreat for awhile, and like David, encourage myself in the Lord.

Satan hates the spread of the gospel, and leadership that helps move people toward a joyful, bold witness of the gospel will often come under attack. In David's case at Ziklag, the women and children had been taken captive, the city had been burned with fire, his army wept till they could weep no more, and some spoke of stoning David. Alone with God, David found encouragement and direction from God to win a great battle and recover all that the Amalekites had taken (I Sam. 30). Sometimes you will have to fight for your joy as well.

Sometimes you will have to fight for your joy

From the autobiography of George Mueller, he says, "It has pleased the Lord to teach me a truth, the benefit of which I have not lost for more than 14 years. The point is this: <u>I saw more clearly than ever the first great and primary business to which I ought to attend every day was to have my soul happy in the Lord.</u> The first thing to be concerned about was not how much I might serve the Lord, or how I might glorify the Lord, <u>but how I might get my soul into a happy state</u>, and how my inner man might be nourished.

<u>How different, when the soul is refreshed and made happy early in the morning, from what it is when, without spiritual preparation, the service, the trials, and the temptations of the day come upon me!</u>"

People are more likely to follow a joyful leader.

In short, **unified, glad, and single-hearted believers make the best evangelists.** They seem to find favour with people, and doors seem to open for them. The Lord loves to add new babies to these joyful nurseries (Acts 2:46, 47).

Pray in the Harvest

Don't miss Jesus' way of keeping people passionate for the harvest. Notice the progression of these familiar words, "The harvest truly is plenteous, but the labourers are few; Pray ye therefore the Lord of the harvest, that He will send forth labourers into His harvest" (Matt. 9:37, 38). This is Christ's way of making our church excellent at outreach. He first wants us, through prayer, to become occupied with the Lord of the harvest. When we do, He pours His life and passion for the shepherdless multitude into us. As we follow Him, He sends us forth into strategic places with sufficient power.

While there, we freely give away what He has freely given to us (Matt. 10:1-8). We never need to evangelize in our own limited strength. We can live by His life and be empowered by His passion for the harvest. **The secret to keep people reaching out is to keep them reaching up.** Jesus is still "moved with compassion," literally "sick to His stomach" over the multitudes. So He instructs us, "Abide in Me, and I in you. As the branch cannot bear fruit of itself, except it abide in the Vine; no more can ye, except ye abide in Me. I am the Vine, ye are the branches. He that abideth in Me and I in him, the same bringeth forth much fruit. For without Me ye can do nothing" (John 15:4, 5).

Without the life-giving Vine, even the most enthusiastic branch will have a very short ministry. As stewards of evangelism, we need to encourage our branches to abide in the Vine, and lasting fruit will come.

We shepherds must minister to their hearts of the sheep so that their hearts will minister through their mouths and proclaim the good news of Jesus. Mark Dever says, "Evangelism, in other words, is not doing everything we can to get a person to make a decision for Jesus—attempting to force a spiritual birth—. Furthermore, evangelism is not the same thing as sharing a personal testimony. It's not the same thing as presenting a rational defense of faith. It's not even doing works of charity, though all three of these things may accompany evangelism. Nor should evangelism be confused with the results of evangelism, as if to say we've only successfully evangelized when a conversion follows. No, evangelism is speaking words. It's sharing news. It's being faithful to God by presenting the good news – that Christ, by His death and resurrection, has secured a way for a holy God and sinful people to be reconciled. God will produce true conversion when we present this good news. In short, evangelism is presenting the good news freely and trusting God to convert people. Salvation comes from the Lord."

The secret to keep people reaching out is to keep them reaching up.

Facilitate Opportunity

I have strongly felt that part of my stewardship at this point is to stay alert to local opportunities for evangelism and bring them to the attention of the congregation. I like to scout things out for them, knowing that prepared hearts will look on their own. Sometimes your approval or caution will encourage them to move out more freely. Here are some common ideas.

1. Teach them to build redemptive relationships with unbelievers.
2. Teach them to use their homes as gospel centers.
3. Give some training in how to give a clear gospel witness.
4. Cast a vision for outreach events where the gospel will be preached. Team evangelism lets even the timid have a part.
5. Teach them how to be alert to divine encounters where a Christian with a prepared heart encounters a lost one who has had God drawing his heart. This is a sweet experience which encourages alertness.
6. Introduce them to local ministries available and looking for volunteers. (Jail ministry, crises pregnancy centers, rest homes, rescue missions, women's shelters, mentoring programs in schools, etc.) Help them see things and reach out.
7. Ordain elders. Be ready to "lay hands" on the faithful and send them forth.

A true reviving from the life of Christ should eventually move us out of our comfort zone into the multitudes with a full heart and a fervent message that Jesus paid it all.

Remember, according to Acts 2:42, the New Testament church believed the same truth (doctrine), they shared the same love (fellowship), they remembered the same gospel (breaking of bread), they were depending on the same source (prayer), and they were committed to the same cause, "to know Christ and make Him known."

Conclusion Section #4

Remember the feature of this section was never meant to be an exhaustive content of each stewardship. Nor was this content meant to offer some mysteriously new material or insight. Much has been written concerning all these stewardships. You are totally capable of adding to each one. My heart here has been to reveal an order which reflects a pattern in the way God, through Jesus, works. In their order, they reflect the ways of God. If we heed them, we can enjoy God's best. Remember that revival is the experience of the church which overflows into evangelism as its expression. Let the servants be glad and press on —

By Grace
Through Faith
In Worship
In Warfare
Through Discipleship
Within the Church
Into the World

SECTION FIVE

The Life of the Vine Forever

.

26
Will It Last?

"To obey is better than sacrifice" –I Samuel 15:22

"Prayer for revival will prevail (only) when it is accompanied by radical amendment of life; not before." –A.W. Tozer

Whether or not revival will last is always the utmost concern of any sincere pastor. In a sense, it is a shade of the reason this book has been written. I will first include the comments of Dr. Erwin Lutzer from his book *Flames of Freedom* in which he gives an account of the Canadian Revival. I would highly recommend this book for students of revival. The following has been taken from his chapter on lasting results as it relates to a revival meeting in a local church or multi-church setting.

DOES REVIVAL LAST? The question is not whether the meetings last, for that would be impossible. Nor is the question whether some of the outward responses to revival continue (e.g., the altar crowded with people every Sunday). That would be quite unnecessary in a church where the believers have learned to walk in fellowship with God daily.

The question is threefold: (1) Are the people who responded remaining true to their commitment to God? (2) Do churches continue on a spirit of revival – honesty, openness, and purity? (3) Are believers now able to witness and to win people to Christ as a result of the revival?

These questions cannot be answered with a yes or no. In some churches involved in the revival the answer to these questions is definitely yes, in some the answer is no, and in the majority it is somewhere in between. Such mixed results follow most revivals. The problem is how to account for those who continue and those who slip back into their former ways.

In the parable of the sower (more accurately called the parable of the soils), Christ vividly taught that the Word of God never receives an equal response from all people. Indeed, if we take the parable quite literally, only one type of soil in four brings forth a bountiful harvest.

Another point emerges. The seed that fell on the shallow, rocky ground was initially the most encouraging to the sower. It sprang up immediately. Imagine how gratified the sower was when he returned a few days after seeding! Yet, in the end, the soil was the most disappointing. Christ explains these people as ones who "when they hear the word, immediately receive it with joy; and they have no firm root in themselves, but are only temporary; then, when affliction or persecution arises because of the word, immediately they fall away" (Mark 4:16b-17).

Sometimes the Word falls on good soil, but eventually the thorns choke it. "These are the ones who have heard the word, and the worries of the world, and the deceitfulness of riches, and the desires for other things enter in and choke the word and it becomes unfruitful" (v. 18b-19).

Similarly, different kinds of people are involved in revival. Some have testified with much joy as to what Christ has done for them, yet after the novelty has worn off, the revival ends for them. Others continue on for a month or a year and then return to their former lifestyle (p. 162-163).

The Reverend Richard Sipley believes that the greatest misconception people have is that after revival the Christian life will be "automatic". If they just keep praising the Lord, they will maintain their high emotional equilibrium. The fact is that no human being can operate at such a high emotional pitch. And it is certainly unnecessary for living a Spirit-controlled life.

Under no conditions, even revival conditions, is it possible to be holy in a hurry.

Sipley points out that Christ, who was always victorious, experienced emotional distress. Ditto for the apostle Paul and other saints of the past who refused to follow their haphazard and unpredictable emotional intuitions (p. 164).

Sometimes people have unrealistic expectations. A prominent marriage counselor observed that a primary reason for unhappy marriages is that couples have unrealistic expectations. They think that marriage will solve all their problems. Some people believe the same about a revival. If the church has problems, they think that revival will solve them completely. They expect believers to mature literally overnight. If all this and more doesn't happen, they turn sour toward revival. One pastor told me, "We've had revival. People were at the altar, but what good did it do? It was a washout." Having people at the altar is no guarantee that they will change. (Sometimes people would rather cry than truly repent!) Also, as already indicated, there must be a follow-through of any basic commitment (p. 165).

Some churches simply get inoculated with revival, that is, they get just enough of it to build up an immunity against it. Their initial exposure prevents them from getting the real thing. To rekindle a spirit of revival in an atmosphere where people have become disappointed in revival is almost impossible. It's like trying to light a fire on grass that has already been burned.

Revival is not a magic cure for the ills of individuals or a church. No revival is a substitute for spiritual vigilance and personal struggle. Considering the strength of the flesh and the devil, we can expect every inch of spiritual progress to be contested.

Those who understand and apply principles of spiritual growth will continue with their new commitment to God. Those who simply are "shopping for a blessing" without being prepared for a life of disciplined study of the Scriptures and prayer will soon be disappointed.

Another problem is that for many people revival is simply cleansing from sin. They have been burdened with guilt, either because they did not understand God's gracious forgiveness or because their conscience was polluted by sins committed against others. Now they experienced the freedom of a clear conscience. But there is a difference between cleansing and learning to walk in the Spirit. An initial experience of joy is not the same as spiritual maturity. **Under no conditions, even revival conditions, is it possible to be holy in a hurry** (p. 166).

Churches where a spirit of revival (i.e., spiritual growth and powerful witness) has continued have certain characteristics. Although there is no "formula" for maintaining vibrant spiritual church life, certain prerequisites are necessary if the church as a whole is to move from dead center into the stream of God's blessing.

The key to the traditional church structure is the pastor. If he is cool toward revival, the church will soon adjust to his temperature. His vision for revival will be an encouragement to the members of the congregation. The Suteras believe that a pastor who spends time in the prayer room during a crusade is more effective in leading his people afterward. He then has his finger on the pulse of the church.

Two other matters are of central importance: structure adjustment and a teaching ministry. First, the structure of the church must adjust to the new life. For example, sharing must continue, though its format might be changed. One pastor observed that, when their sharing dried up, "We ended up talking to ourselves about ourselves." To expect that sharing will continue as it did during the revival is unrealistic. The revival brought major spiritual breakthroughs; presumably, when believers learn to walk in the Spirit day by day, their accounts of victory will not be as dramatic as those experienced during revival.

How can meaningful sharing continue? The answer, I believe, is that the focal point of sharing must be the Scriptures. Out of the context of informal Bible studies and prayer, needs will surface. A climate of honesty and acceptance must be established so that the believers learn to "keep short accounts with God" (p. 176).

... People have their lives cleansed, and a spirit of openness prevails. Then later the doors of their lives are closed, they become complacent, and soon their lives are cluttered with the rubbish of the world.

"How long does your basement stay clean?" Sipley asks. Rubbish, as we know, can accumulate rapidly. Our only recourse is to keep the temple open. We must be real people, giving an honest picture of our spiritual complexion.

This can be best done in small groups. George Webber, in his book (*The Congregation in Mission*), argues that small groups should be the basic unit in the life of a congregation. He writes, "A new structure of congregational life is called for which makes provision for genuine meetings between persons, a context in which the mask of self-deception and distrust will be maintained only with difficulty and in which men and women will begin to relate to each other at the level of their true humanity in Christ."

Webber effectively argues that people who have listened politely to sermons for years "are most likely to squirm in the face of honest confrontation and only with difficulty can they brush aside the demands upon their lives."

Group interaction should not be something just added onto the traditional church program. It is not an optional appendage which can be tacked on when the occasion calls for it. The climate of openness and honesty and the experience of weeping with those that weep and rejoicing with those that rejoice ought to become a way of life. For revival to continue, the atmosphere of revival must continue. Not an emotional atmosphere, but an honest one. Such a climate prevails in churches where the revival continues.

Second, spiritual doldrums often following revival can be overcome only by a strong teaching ministry. Now is not the time to preach inspirational sermonettes designed to recreate the highly charged emotional atmosphere of revival. Rather, it is the time for solid doctrine: justification, sanctification, and the ministries of the Holy Spirit. The objective truths must be stressed, since they are the foundation of our experience.

After the revival some pastors used sharing as a cop-out for intensive sermon preparation and Bible study. They expected that sharing would take the place of teaching. The results were disastrous. The revival "fizzled out" when people expected the revival to continue on its own steam.

Any church that expects to coast on the momentum of revival is due for a bitter surprise. ... **No church needs sound doctrine more than a revived one ....** Teaching and discipleship must have top priority.

Does revival last? Yes, the effects of revival last. Some churches were spared from oblivion as a result of the revival. Even where a church as a whole did not maintain a spirit of revival, there are individuals within the congregation who date the beginning of their commitment to God to the days of revival. As one critic remarked, "I have to admit that even four years later, there are still people whose lives are irrevocably changed as a result of what happened."

No church needs sound doctrine more than a revived one.

After speaking to scores of people involved in the revival both in Canada and the United States, I can vouch for this fact: there are hundreds of people who gladly testify that revival was for them the beginning of a new way of life (p. 172).

Does revival last? If revival is God's work in bringing the church to New Testament Christianity, the revival will last as long as we want it to! If purity, love, and power are the earmarks of the body of Christ, indeed, such characteristics ought to last. If not, we – not God – have failed (p. 174).

Let me tie Dr. Lutzer's comments to the premise of this book, i.e., Revival happens when we practice the presence of Christ through Scripture-based (expository preferred) preaching and praying and allow Him to be actively in charge of our lives and our church. All reviving life comes from one life, the resurrected life of Christ through the Holy Spirit. He is the life of the Vine in the soul of the church.

The object of our faith for reviving is the person of Jesus. All the stewardships to lasting revival have Him at the center. A constant surrender to His authority and activity postures the church to enjoy a lifestyle of revival.

Tozer says it well. "We hear much discussion about revival and renewal. People talk about spiritual power in the churches. I think this fact – this truth – that Jesus Christ wants to be known in His church as the ever-living, never changing Lord of all could bring back again the power and the testimony of the early church."

I wonder if you feel like me when, I survey much of Christendom in today's world: "They have taken away my Lord and do not know what they have done with Him!" If we

<blockquote>
The object of our faith for reviving is the person of Jesus.
</blockquote>

would only seek and welcome our Lord's presence in our midst, we would have the assurance that He is the same Lord He has always been!

I agree. If Jesus is our revival then reviving will continue. It must!

27

What Does a God-Centered Stewardship Look Like?

"And let them make me a sanctuary; that I may dwell among them. According to all that I shew thee after the pattern of the tabernacle, and the pattern of all the instruments thereof, even so shall ye make it." –Exodus 25:8, 9

"The building of the tabernacle is a clear and classic illustration of how to start with God and end with God in our stewardship." –jch

The instructions given to Moses by God in the building of the tabernacle are a flawless model of how we can allow God to build and still be humanly responsible in our leadership.

First of all, Moses was an amazing, God-centered prophet, Israel's greatest, because God chose to meet with him face to face. God came to Moses' defense when Aaron and Miriam spoke against him. Note God's witness of Moses.

"'Hear now My words; if there is a prophet among you, I the Lord will make Myself known unto him in a vision, and will speak unto him in a dream. **My servant Moses is not so,** who is faithful in all <u>Mine</u> house. With him will I speak mouth to mouth, (face to face) even apparently (plainly), and not in dark speeches; – wherefore then were ye not afraid to speak against my servant Moses?' And the anger of the Lord was kindled against them;" –Numbers 12:6-9

Similar statements are made in Exodus 33:11 and Deuteronomy 34:10. Such a stellar, God-authored commendation of leadership demands our observation. God spoke to Moses without mediation. Also, the Lord did not speak to Moses through visions and dreams but plainly. It was not that Moses saw the full glory of God, but rather that he had the most explicit, intimate encounters, above those of any other prophet. In response to these encounters, God said, "He is faithful in all My house." That's what we are after in our leadership: Intimate in our communication; Immaculate in our obedience.

Secondly, the tabernacle was a God-centered project strategic to Israel's health, safety, and progress as a nation. The tabernacle was the way Israel could be <u>camping out with God</u> on their pilgrimage. Through this tent of meeting God gave Israel seven messages from His heart.

1. I want to be with you.
2. I want to cleanse you.
3. I want to protect you.
4. I want to move with you.
5. I want things done My way.
6. I have an end in mind.
7. I have another prophet like Moses, i.e., Jesus.

The tabernacle was the way Israel could be <u>camping out with God</u> on their pilgrimage.

Our churches and the tabernacle are not one and the same, but the integrity of their construction is. Both should start with God and end with God. Here are God's divine instructions to this genuinely meek prophet for the erection of this physical prototype of Jesus. Observe carefully.

Through the finished tabernacle, God gives us His message (heart), but in the building of the tabernacle, He demonstrates His method (hand). Here they are in order. We —

1. Start with God's glory (Ex. 24:16, 17). Moses and company were pilgrims. They had no glory of their own. Neither do we. This leads us to —

2. Seek God's presence (Ex. 24:12, 13, 18). God said, "Come up to Me into the mount, and be there;" The idea here is that of an unending appointment. Direction for holy leadership cannot be rushed. We know now that it was a forty-day visit, but Moses didn't know that at the time. When we are building reflections of Jesus, we need time to get them right. We all have had first-hand experience in how these "first appointments" have to be fought for and kept with all diligence both privately and corporately. The way of a healthy church is to have strategic sessions with the Master Builder. There we—

3. Receive God's project (Ex. 24:12b; 25:8). "and I will give thee tables of stone and a law, and commandments which I have written; that thou mayest teach them" (24:12). "And let them make me a sanctuary; that I may dwell among them" (25:8).

Notice these projects were received by Moses and given by God. They were not the products of a "brain storming" session. Good ideas are not always God's ideas. John the Baptist securely reported as his ministry was falling behind Jesus's: "A man can receive nothing unless it has been given to him from heaven" (Jn. 3:27).

It is comforting to observe God's desire to give Israel both His Word and His presence. The means of bringing that to our people will be birthed in God's presence through His projects. After which we —

4. Wait on God's provision (Ex. 25:1-7; 36:5-7). The specific needs were outlined by God, and the supply came from willing, generous hearts. Not everyone gave, and those who did gave from the spoils they gleaned from their exit from Egypt. Remember, they were pilgrims. Their hearts

embraced the project so much that Moses had to restrain the giving. When God's heart is in the project, He will raise up people with the same heart. We can't be in a hurry. The process is as important to God as the end product. Be patient, and the "invisible supply" will appear in God's time. In the meantime, we —

5. Follow God's pattern (Ex. 25:9, 40; 26:30, 27:8). God has a way He wants things done. His insistence about this with Moses is notable. Strategy matters to God. Wood, hay and stubble are real and will be burned. Moses inspected all the work to make sure it was done just as the Lord had commanded (Ex. 39:43). With this willingness to be given to detail, he received a good report from God that he was "faithful in all <u>Mine</u> house." We are ministers (servants) of Christ and stewards of the mysteries of God. "Moreover, it is required in stewards that a man be found faithful" (I Cor. 4:2). We must then —

6. Employ God's personnel (Ex. 31:1-6). I've got to believe when God was giving those precise instructions for the tabernacle to Moses with all of the "Thou shalt makes," he could have been thinking. "And who is going to do this?" Growing up in the palace and then caring for sheep didn't necessarily equip Moses in the trades. But God, as always, had a plan to provide His leader with gifted, passionate partners. These words from God must have brought great relief to Moses. Listen to them carefully.

"See, I have called by name Bezaleel — and I have filled him with the Spirit of God, in wisdom, and in understanding, and in knowledge, and in all manner of workmanship, to devise cunning works, to work in gold, and in silver, and in brass, and in cutting of stones, to set them, and in carving of timber, to work in all manner of workmanship. And I, behold, I have given with him Aholiab —: and in the hearts of all that are wise hearted I have put wisdom, that they may make all that I have commanded thee."

I am choking up as I write this because I have experienced first-hand how the God who ordained the message and the manner in which it was presented also raised up the materials for the project and the men to put it together. It's fantastic! There needs to be an integrity about our waiting on God that allows us to realize who He is calling. They are—

7. Motivated by God's power (31:3). My mentors in revival encouraged me to learn the difference between good men, church men and Spirit-appointed men. These kinds are not always found amongst the seminary grads or shrewd business executives. Note also that competence and character can come in the same package. Be assured that bad staff is worse than no staff at all. Wait on God. He has someone in mind, and he may be nestled in your own congregation.

There came a time in our ministry when we discovered that the best ministers for us were those who were growing up with us. They often came from the faithful who weathered well the storms we had gone through. Your attitude as a leader will make a great difference in whether or not your men and women even want to join the team. It is so invigorating to watch God put in the heart of your own flock a desire to join the cause. Note the words God used here: Spirit of God, wisdom, understanding, knowledge, all manner of workmanship, devise cunning works. And God repeatedly said that He would put all this in them! We need to wait and look for the Bezaleels and the Aholiabs who lead the wise-hearted to build all that God has commanded. Those who then —

8. Serve for God's glory (39:30, 32) The following words describe the final movements of the hands of the craftsmen.
"And they made the plate of the holy crown pure of gold, and wrote upon it a writing, like to the engravings of a signet, HOLINESS TO THE LORD."

The artists did not inscribe the piece with their own name. They signed God's name. They credited the real artist. How different our ministries when the staff and laborers intentionally serve for God's glory. You know what happens when we live like this? God signs His name to us. Notice, "Thus was all the work of the tabernacle of the tent of the congregation finished: and the children of Israel did according to all that the Lord commanded Moses, so did they" (v. 32). "And Moses did look upon all the work, and, behold, they had done it as the Lord had commanded, even so had they done it: and Moses blessed them" (v. 43).

Knowing neither the full reason behind all the details, nor the end of the story, these pilgrims simply obeyed and received a "well done" from God and Moses.

The crowning moment of this endeavor is described in Exodus 40:34, 35.

> "Then a cloud covered the tent of the congregation, and the glory of the Lord filled the tabernacle. And Moses was not able to enter into the tent of the congregation, because the cloud abode thereon, and the glory of the Lord filled the tabernacle."

> God was obviously present and actively in charge. God chose to dwell with them, to be seen by them, and to go with them throughout all their journeys. God always finishes what He sets out to do, and God always does it right the first time. This is what any ministry can expect when we start with God's glory and end with God's glory.

Without elaboration from me, take time to compare this glory with the tragedy that comes when a people decide to operate independently from God and mold their own calf (Ex. 32).

> "For of Him, and through Him, and to Him,
> are all things: to whom be glory forever.
> Amen," (Rom. 11:36).

28
The Church that Jesus Builds

*"— he that sanctifieth and they who are
sanctified are all one: for which cause
he is not ashamed to call them brethren
saying 'I will declare thy name unto my
brethren, in the midst of the church will
I sing praise unto thee."* –Hebrews 2:11, 12

"When Jesus is given His proper place by the church,
He will bring His song to the church." –jch

Our introductory verse is a quote from Psalm which reflects the heart of the Messiah which was to come. The first 21 verses characterize the lament of a Messiah forsaken, while the last 10 verses are the praise of a Messiah found. It was applied immediately to David and ultimately to Jesus. So Hebrews 2:12 are the words of Jesus in the assembly. (church) **Did you ever think about Jesus wanting to express Himself in your church? Is that possible? How does it work?**

Jesus had taught that those who do the will of the Father in obedience to His Word are His brothers and sisters and mother (Matt. 12:50; Luke 8:21). After the resurrection, He directly called the disciples "brethren" (Matt. 28:10, John 20:17). When He had paid the price for their salvation, they truly became His spiritual brothers and sisters. The use of the term demonstrates His full identification with mankind in order to provide complete redemption. According to this Scripture, He says we are one, He calls us brethren, and He wants to declare the name of the Father to us and sing praise to the Father in the midst of our assembly.

The idea agrees perfectly with the Apostle Paul's prayer for the Ephesians in Ephesians 3. In verses 14-21, he prayed for this church that God would grant to them strength according to the riches of His glory by His Spirit in the inner man. He prayed that Christ would dwell in their hearts and feel right at home. He longed for them to know the immeasurable, four-dimensional love of Jesus and be filled with all the fullness of God. He ends his prayer with this blessing.

"Now unto Him that is able to do exceeding abundantly above all that we ask or think, according to the power that worketh in us, unto Him be glory in the church by Christ Jesus throughout all ages, world without end. Amen," (Eph. 4:20-21).

When the Son is free to give praise to the Father in our assembly through our love and the stories of the redeemed, we have a healthy, living church. Even the children sense it.

With that being said, let's walk through the New Testament with Jesus as our tour guide and let Him point to the qualities of the church He works with us to build. Here they are in the first person.

Matthew 16:13-19
• I will build My church upon My own person and work.

Matthew 18:15-20
• I will give to My church My presence for conflict resolution.

Matthew 28:18-20
• I will give the church My authority to make disciples.
• I will work with My church and remain in them.

Acts 13:1-3
• I will call ministers from My church and give them ministries that I have ordained for them.

Ephesians 2:19-22

- My church is the dwelling place of God in the Spirit.

Ephesians 3:14-21

- My church is limited only by My sovereignty.

Ephesians 4:11-16

- I give leaders to My church who will equip the saints who will then work in ministry to edify the body.
- Through this process I will build the spiritual health of My body.

Ephesians 5:23-33

- I am the head of My church (v. 23).
- I am her Savior (v. 23).
- My church is subject to Me (v. 24).
- I love My church (v. 25).
- I gave Myself for My church (v. 25).
  (To sanctify, to cleanse, to present to Myself glorious, no spots, no wrinkles, Holy, without blemish)
- I nourish and cherish My church (v. 29).
- My church is My body on earth (v. 30).
- My church is a mystery (v. 32).

I Timothy 3:15

- My church is the pillar and ground of the truth in society.

Revelation 1:16

- I hold the pastors for My church in My hand.

Revelation 2 & 3

- I know My church intimately.
- I have the answers for My church.
- I have My church's best interest in mind.

- I have the right and ability to remove the witness of My church.
- I know the conditions around My church.

Revelation 22:16
- The unveiling of who I am is to be testified in My church.

As a steward, feel free to add your insights to these qualities. Anything we can do to encourage our affections for this "Elect Lady" and her Builder will affect the ages. **The fact that Jesus nourishes and cherishes His church should be a call on our lives to do the same.**

The fact that Jesus nourishes and cherishes His church should be a call on our lives to do the same.

"Do you hear them coming, brother,
Thronging up the steeps of light,
Clad in glorious shining garments –
Blood washed garments pure and white?

'Tis a glorious church without spot or
wrinkle, washed in the blood of the Lamb." –R.E. Hudson

A Closing Word to Stewards

We believe the Living Word (Jesus) and the written Word (Bible) are supernatural and are our only hope for transforming lives for eternal salvation and the glory of God.

We believe this transforming gospel has been given to the church as an entrusted stewardship. Through the church, God gets glory by Jesus Christ. He is our active Head and only foundation. The uniting of worldwide ethnic groups from every tribe and nation through the redemption and indwelling of the resurrected Christ is a sure hope, yet a mystery, hidden from us in ages past.

It's not easy to be a steward of this mystery because its Kingdom has so many invisible aspects. It is often soft spoken, and its Spirit is not heard unless ears have been prepared which immediately makes us branch-like stewards totally dependent and desperate for the Vine. Quickly we learn that without Him, we can do nothing. Only He can produce lasting fruit.

Even with all these difficulties and "glass darklies," we are admonished to get good at our stewardship and be faithful. **It is vital to remember that only what is done under Christ's authority brings glory to God.** There are many subtle substitutes for Jesus, and they must not be allowed to take center stage. Not even our attempts to be intentional. Even revival itself can become our focus and not Jesus. Our enemy is fine with anything that takes the place of Jesus. We become what we behold. Therefore, our beholding must be nothing but Jesus.

This mystery was birthed from God long before we came on the scene and will continue long after our watch is over. It will be solved in a consummation beyond our imagination, but we can be thankful that we had a part.

To our ministries, God has entrusted the greatest power of the universe past, present, and future – the power of the resurrected life of Christ. He is the life of the Vine in the soul of His church. He has

It is vital to remember that only what is done under Christ's authority brings glory to God.

given us the authority, i.e., the right to use that power to make disciples of Jesus for the glory of God. No matter how powerfully dark and corrupt the world system is determined to become, still greater is He who is in us than he who is in the world.

So as you have received this stewardship by grace, embrace it by faith. Continue in worship and warfare. Pour your life into those who stay faithful. Train them in ministry within the body, then release them into the world. This is how we let Christ build His church while maintaining responsible leadership. Abiding in the Vine and with the Vine is not good advice, it's good news. See you at the Throne.

In Him,
Joe

After-Glow

One of my favorite elements of God's reviving is the sharing of testimonies. After the meetings were dismissed, people were invited to stay and share what God was doing. Sometimes testimonies would last for two hours. They became a real source of encouragement. What the preachers were saying in their messages was now being repeated by changed lives. Here is a sampling of current testimonies from those who are still going strong in their faith and freedom. Enjoy —

The false masks that we had worn for so long were thrown on the heap of hypocrisy littering the floor of the church auditorium. It was a beautiful, life-altering experience. We no longer pretended to have it all together. We told our stories and were loved and forgiven in spite of them. We no longer played church. We became the church.

Craig and Granda

Our Pastor Dr. Gregg Curtis announced that Life Action Ministries from Michigan would be coming for two weeks of meetings. Two weeks of planned nightly meetings seemed like a long commitment. I was skeptical of why, but after a few evenings, God showed up. He found us. I am sure people had prayed ahead of time for these meetings, but it seemed like He showed up – He found us.

Some people found Jesus and salvation. Others were Christians who found victories over long time hurts and sin. Many found liberation to their souls. It was VERY transparent in its outward manifestation.

It was the only true revival I have ever experienced. I have been in other meetings called revival but they were just meetings, profitable teaching and encouragement. The true revival was God with us, moving hearts and souls, touching people deeply. It was exciting and completely real.

Barbara

There were so many things that the Spirit of God graciously opened my eyes to during the time of revival in our church – the fact that we humanize God and deify man, the root of all my sin is pride, just for starters. However, as I think back, one of the most surprising revelations for me was the night they spoke on sins of the spirit. They went through several examples as I rather self-righteously checked the items off my "not guilty" list, until they came to the sin of the critical spirit. While I was quick to mentally check this sin off also, there was a check in my spirit. God in His kindness gently prodded my thinking as examples of a critical spirit were discussed. While I would consider myself fairly upbeat and positive most of the time, God had brought a very challenging situation into my life – someone new in leadership that was changing everything and had some values that were very different from mine. I won't go into all the details, and suffice it to say, I had developed a very critical spirit. The reason it wasn't so obvious to me initially is because I was quite sure my feelings were justified. During the course of the Holy Spirit illuminating my eyes and heart to see my real attitude, I sensed the Lord was gently rebuking me saying, "I opened your eyes to his flaws so that you would lift him up to me regularly. He is my child and growing…just like you." Since then many times when I am finding a critical spirit within, God brings my thoughts back to that lesson. It was really life changing. Thank You, Jesus.

Jan

Revival, as God was finally able to show me, is not a congregational event, at least in its beginning. It is a meeting between each individual and his Redeemer, predicated on a platform of complete and total honesty, confession, repentance, and bathed in prayer. It was a resolve to keep walls that I had constructed protecting me from conviction, confession and repentance from being reconstructed!

For me, I expect to lose the occasional battle but am certain of the victory in the war, because it was won at Calvary. Life Action has helped me to realize revival needs to occur in me every day! Being prepared, available and willing to proclaim the Truth—Jesus is Lord.

Dave

In about 1985, we experienced financial problems and lost a business we had worked diligently to make work. It was God's timing for a friend to invite us to a Life Action meeting in a local church. God was what we needed and He had proved to be faithful. We began hearing things we had not been taught in the past: how the borrower is servant to the lender, relationships, and making God the center of our lives. To seek God first in all things and He needs to be involved in our decisions. Another thing we learned is that sin does not have power over us.

Even though we could have lost our home and farm, God allowed us to sell a portion of it. It was like He was saying, "I am making a way if you will just give up a part of what you have." He has provided so richly for us and given us three daughters and sons-in-law and nine grandchildren. We are doing what we can to pass on what we have learned to keep them from making those mistakes. We are thankful that He is our Provider. We know that God's Word changed us and God used Life Action to teach us the truth.

Loren and Janice

It's been about 30 years now since Life Action Ministries came to the church I was attending. It was not uncommon for us to have different groups in and I did not expect this group to be any different. One of the first examples used started a change in my life that is still working in me today. It was an orange and what happens when you poke a hole in it and squeeze it. What comes out is what is inside, not too hard to understand. But applying that to my life I saw that even though I had accepted Christ over ten years before, the "old man" was very much alive and well in my heart. When the pressure was applied what came out many times was not Christ. Since that time seeing how I really am, is not how I want others to see me, has been a concern of my heart.

Don

When Life Action Revival came to our church thirty-one years ago, it had a lasting result in our lives. My husband was 28 and I was 25, expecting our second child. I had accepted Christ as my Savior as a child, and grew up in the church. My husband was saved during his senior year in high school. God was good to us, and we married in our early twenties. We were busy serving in our local church where my husband was a deacon, taught Sunday school class and all seemed well. A few nights into the revival my husband began to be under deep conviction. The conviction was so heavy he could not even work. His first thought was that he must not really be saved, but after praying for God to save him, he had no relief. After one of the revival services he was encouraged to write down all of the sins he could think of. All of those were hidden from me and others. Some were smaller issues and some were bigger strongholds. He confessed them all to God and men, and after making restitution for some, God gave him a freedom that he had never experienced before! I had a husband that had so much joy for the Lord! One thing he always said that he had learned from that time was, "to keep short sin accounts!" He has lived that out in his life and taught it to our children. He has been a godly husband and father to our children, and now grandchildren. During that time I understood more how to love my husband and experience a daily relationship with Christ. We have both fell in love with His Word and have learned to trust God no matter what!

Dave and Becky

"Consider the work of God; for who can make that straight, which He hath made crooked?" (Eccl. 7:13). The 1985 revival was a crucial period for me and my three children. I had asked the Lord to cause me to be more compassionate not knowing that my entire world would be disrupted through a broken marriage. Through those days God showed me a new way of grace, faith and hope which allowed me to know Him better and truly become His daughter. This brokenness and refreshing continues to transform me into Christlikeness.

My present husband and I are blessed beyond measure and are surrounded daily by His love. Through the revival, my three children were secured in their faith causing them to put the Lord first in ministering to their families. Truly the study of God's Word has sustained us through the crooked and the straight.

Pam

Dear Pastor,

Time alone has prevented me from gleaning more examples of ongoing revival in people's lives. These few are a very small sampling of people who became team members with me in ministering to others. They are an example of stewarding the results of God's moving. May you also continue to train and encourage those God gives you, whether their reviving came from a special meeting or simply meeting God on their own in His Word. Be confident that what God has begun He will perform until the day of Jesus Christ.

Confident in Him,
Joe

The Life of the Vine in the Soul of the Church – 7 Stewardships of Revival

Notes

Chapter 4:   *Biblical Preaching; Haddon Robinson*, page 20

Chapter 12:   *The Cross and Christian Ministry*, D.A. Carson, page 9
The Crucified King, Dr. Jeremy Treat, page 37

Chapter 19:   *The Covington/Danville Revival-Article*
Spirit of Revival; Life Action Ministries, volume 1, number 2, August 1985
Matthew Henry Commentary–volume 5, page 377

Chapter 26:   *Flames of Freedom*, Erwin Lutzer, Moody Press, pages 162-174

A recommended companion book:
The Power of Praying Together,
Oliver Price, Kregel Publishers

The Life of the Vine in the Soul of the Church – 7 Stewardships of Revival

Joe Humrichous (jch) is a pastor and conference speaker. He is currently the Executive Director of Bible Prayer Fellowship Midwest and a pastor at First Baptist Church in Covington, Indiana. He is a graduate of Pillsbury Baptist Bible College, with a Bachelor of Arts degree, and Temple Baptist Theological Seminary, with a Master of Divinity.

Joe and his wife, Teresa, have a blended family of five grown children and 13 grandchildren and reside in West Lebanon, Indiana.

Connect with Joe:
P.O. Box 567
West Lebanon, IN 47991
Cell: 217.304.4741
joehumrichous@yahoo.com
Paradigm1.org